CHOCOLATES
— AND —
SWEETS

Front cover photograph by Dave Jordan
shows a selection of chocolates

Published 1986 on behalf of
The Boots Company Plc Nottingham England
by Hamlyn Publishing
Bridge House, London Road, Twickenham,
Middlesex, England

Copyright © Hamlyn Publishing 1986
a division of The Hamlyn Publishing Group Ltd

ISBN 0 600 32612 8

Set in 10/11pt Gill Sans Light
by Photocomp Ltd, Birmingham

Printed in Italy

Contents

Useful Facts & Figures

Notes on metrication

In this book quantities are given in metric and Imperial measures. Exact conversion from Imperial to metric measures does not usually give very convenient working quantities and so the metric measures have been rounded off into units of 25 grams. The table below shows the recommended equivalents.

Ounces	Approx g to nearest whole figure	Recommended conversion to nearest unit of 25
1	28	25
2	57	50
3	85	75
4	113	100
5	142	150
6	170	175
7	198	200
8	227	225
9	255	250
10	283	275
11	312	300
12	340	350
13	368	375
14	396	400
15	425	425
16 (1 lb)	454	450
17	482	475
18	510	500
19	539	550
20 (1¼ lb)	567	575

Note: When converting quantities over 20 oz first add the appropriate figures in the centre column, then adjust to the nearest unit of 25. As a general guide, 1 kg (1000 g) equals 2·2 lb or about 2 lb 3 oz. This method of conversion gives good results in nearly all cases, although in certain pastry and cake recipes a more accurate conversion is necessary to produce a balanced recipe.

Liquid measures The millilitre has been used in this book and the following table gives a few examples.

Imperial	Approx ml to nearest whole figure	Recommended ml
¼ pint	142	150 ml
½ pint	283	300 ml
¾ pint	425	450 ml
1 pint	567	600 ml
1½ pints	851	900 ml
1¾ pints	992	1000 ml (1 litre)

Spoon measures All spoon measures given in this book are level unless otherwise stated.

Can sizes At present, cans are marked with the exact (usually to the nearest whole number) metric equivalent of the Imperial weight of the contents, so we have followed this practice when giving can sizes.

Note: *When making any of the recipes in this book, only follow one set of measures as they are not interchangeable.*

Sugar Boiling

Without a sugar thermometer Have a basin or cup of cold water available and drop in a small quantity of the mixture to see which stage has been reached.

With a sugar thermometer Allow the mixture to boil in the pan for a minute or two after the sugar has thoroughly dissolved. Put in the thermometer and gently move this around in the mixture. This gives you an overall and accurate reading. Try to read the thermometer quickly and without lifting it too far out of the sugar mixture, for the temperature drops rapidly when the thermometer is removed.

Whether you are testing with or without a thermometer, remove the pan from the heat as you test or take the reading, and do not replace on the heat unless you are satisfied further cooking is necessary.

Temperatures and appearance

Description	Temperature °C	°F	Appearance
Thread	107.2 to 108.8	225 to 228	The syrup is so thin that it runs off the spoon into the cold water. If kept on the spoon for a moment and pinched, it forms a hot substance. A stage rarely used in sweet-making except as a sticking coating. For a firmer coating boil to 108.8 C/228 F.
Pearl	110 to 111.6	230 to 233	The syrup forms tiny pearl-like balls in the cold water, too soft to form a sweetmeat. This stage is used occasionally for binding or coating ingredients.
Blow	112.7	235	The bubbles float when tested in cold water. A continuation of the pearl stage, not a sweetmeat stage.

Temperatures and appearance

Description	Temperature °C	°F	Appearance
Soft Ball	114.4 to 115.5	238 to 240	When the sweet mixture drops into the cold water it can be gathered up and formed into a soft ball with the fingers. Used for fudge and other sweetmeats; fondant mixtures are boiled to a slightly higher temperature.
Firm Ball	118.3 to 121.1	245 to 250	The sugar mixture can be formed into a pliable, but firmer ball at this temperature. Used for caramels. A firmer ball (or 'light crack') is made by increasing the temperatures up to 126.6-132.2 C/260-270 F. Between 132.2-138 C/270-280 F, there is a stage which has no particular characteristics.
Crack	138 to 143.3	280 to 290	In the crack stage the sugar mixture will break quite easily between your fingers. This temperature is used for certain toffees or sweets like butterscotch; the crack stage continues up to the next stage, the higher the temperature the more brittle the mixture
Caramel	155.5 to 177	312 to 350	At this stage the sugar mixture begins to change colour drastically; it caramelises – not to be confused with caramels. Care must be taken not to exceed this for if the sugar mixture boils above this stage it becomes over-brown, then blackens. Too dark a caramel tastes bitter and unpalatable; any temperature above 177 C/350 F makes the caramel too dark.

Sugar Lollies (page 52)

Introduction

To many people reading this book, the art of making chocolates, Easter eggs or other sweets may well be an entirely new form of cooking. I am confident though that you will discover that preparing confectionery of various kinds is not only easy but both a satisfying and money-saving occupation too. You will be able to make sweets and chocolates with a real homemade flavour for your family, or produce enjoyable and original presents for your friends. You may well be able to use your skill at making sweets as a means of raising money for your favourite charity.

Before you begin any of the recipes I would suggest you read this and the next page, dealing with the choice of ingredients, and then the following pages which describe the kind of equipment used in making chocolates and confectionery.

I have covered a wide range of recipes in the book. The first pages show how to prepare a chocolate coating; this is followed by numerous suggestions for making your own chocolates. If you do this you can select just the fillings you or your friends enjoy most, so that every box of chocolates will be full of favourites. Following these recipes you will find information on the correct techniques for producing your own Easter eggs or enchanting small chocolate animals or figures.

After the selection of chocolate and truffle recipes come ideas for making a variety of toffees, boiled sweets, fudge, candies, nougat, marshmallows and jellied sweets. When you feel you have insufficent time to prepare cooked sweets then try some of the uncooked delights. These taste delicious and only you will know how easy they have been to produce.

A History of Chocolate

Chocolate is an essential ingredient in many recipes. Homemade chocolates are probably the most popular, and certainly the most luxurious, of all forms of confectionery, and yet you can make them at home with little effort.

The history of chocolate can be traced back through the centuries. Although the Western world did not discover the delights of drinking chocolate until the mid 17th century, it had certainly been appreciated by the Aztecs some hundreds of years before the Spanish conquest of these people in the early 16th century. The name 'chocolate' is attributed either to the Aztec 'schoco' and 'latté' or the Mexican 'chocolatl'. This means 'bitter water' and it indicates that the first chocolate drinks were less sweet and appealing than those made today.

The origin of chocolate lies in the bean pods of the cocoa tree, botanically known as 'Theobroma Cacao'. These trees now grow in many parts of the world. The beans are removed from the bean pods and are then allowed to ferment for some days; after this they are dried to produce cocoa nibs. These nibs contain a certain amount of cocoa butter, but real chocolate is produced by blending extra cocoa butter and sugar with the cocoa nibs. In some instances milk is added to give the less strongly flavoured milk chocolate. There are a number of variations on the market from which you can choose when preparing your own homemade chocolates or chocolate shapes. Always buy the best quality available from good manufacturers, for cheap chocolate has been produced from inferior cocoa beans and this is reflected in both the taste and texture.

CHOICE OF CHOCOLATE

When making confectionery at home, there is a wide range of chocolate to choose from, varying in colour, flavour and quality. Select from the following, according to taste and to best suit the recipe.

Bitter chocolate is similar to plain chocolate, but as it contains less sugar it is not a general favourite. It is however excellent as a dipping chocolate, especially for very sweet centres.

Plain chocolate, which is readily available, is an excellent choice for coating fillings or for making moulds. It is moderately sweet, so will please most people, and yet it has sufficiently strong taste to form a good contrast to any rich or sweet fillings. It is excellent in baking too.

Milk chocolate can be used in sweet-making. Particular care must be taken when melting this to make sure it does not become overheated. It is a favourite with many children.

Chocolate couverture is often known as 'dipping' or 'coating' chocolate. It is of high quality and is produced in two types, i.e. light (milk) or dark. This chocolate has a high fat content, so that it retains a pleasant shine, even after melting. It may not be sufficiently sweet for all tastes.

Chocolate menier has a greater cocoa content than plain chocolate, so it is both darker in colour and stronger in taste. It can be used in sweet-making, provided you are sure that everyone will enjoy the flavour.

Chocolate cake coverings are obtainable in both plain and milk chocolate flavours. These are not suitable for making chocolates. As the name suggests they are manufactured to be melted and then used as a covering on cakes. They are produced from vegetable fats, sugar and flavouring. In some cases they may include a certain amount of cocoa.

Cocoa powder and drinking chocolate powder (this has a percentage of sugar added to the cocoa powder) can be successfully used in some sweets.

White chocolate is ideal for coating fruits or for other confectionery. It is available as chocolate couverture, chocolate drops or in bars. It is produced by using the cocoa butter, which is creamy white in colour, instead of brown cocoa.

You can buy chocolate products in various forms:
Blocks of chocolate are the most usual; these should be broken into pieces or grated to facilitate melting.

Chocolate drops or buttons are produced from good plain or milk chocolate. They can be used for decoration or for melting. Their small size makes them very practical for this purpose. You may be able to buy loose chocolate pieces from a confectioner.

Chocolate strands, sometimes called chocolate nonpareils or vermicelli, are ideal for decoration and for coating some truffles and other sweets. They are made from sugar and flavourings.

OTHER INGREDIENTS

Fats: unsalted butter is the ideal fat for sweet-making, but margarine can be substituted in some recipes (this will be indicated in the recipe). When tins are brushed to prevent the sweets sticking as they set, you should use melted butter or a very good quality olive or corn oil; be sparing with the amounts used, so you do not spoil the surface of the sweets.

Flavourings: these are provided in various ways. They can be the fillings in chocolates or the fruit and nuts in fudge. Alcohol is used in liqueur chocolates and in some sweets too. Flavouring essences should be used sparingly and added to the mixture in the same way as colouring, drop by drop from the skewer.

Fruit: dried fruit is an important ingredient in many sweets. If the fruit seems a little too dry you can take some of the liquid from the recipe (as in the case of fudge or toffee), put this with the fruit in a basin and leave for 1 to 2 hours. Then strain off the liquid, use it in the recipe and add the moistened fruit when indicated in the cooking process. However, you cannot moisten dried fruit if it is to be blended with melted chocolate, so choose fruit for this purpose carefully.

Milk and cream: recipes will indicate the type of cream that is recommended. You achieve far better results by using full-cream canned or fresh milk in fudge and similar recipes. This has the added advantage that the higher fat content helps to prevent it sticking to the pan.

Nuts: many nuts are used in sweet-making. In most cases these need to be blanched, which means that the skins should be removed. Almonds are now sold ready skinned, but if you have unskinned almonds, or pistachios, put these into boiling water, leave for 30-60 seconds then remove from the water and pull off the skins. Dry the nuts well before using. Other nuts, like Brazils and hazelnuts, should be heated for about 4 to 5 minutes in a moderately hot oven (190 C, 375 F, gas 5). You will then find it quite easy to slip off the skins.

Sweetening: granulated sugar is ideal for many sweets but in some cases a different sugar is specified. Golden syrup and black treacle (or molasses) are other ingredients used in sweet-making. A standard tablespoon measure gives 25 g/1 oz syrup or treacle.

You can however weigh the syrup or treacle if you first weigh the pan in which the sweet is to be cooked, then add the correct weight of syrup or treacle with the pan still on the scales.

Other additions: colourings are often put into sweets to make them more appealing, but these are not essential. Choose the best quality available and add the colouring gradually by dipping the tip of a skewer into the bottle and allowing the drops to fall off it into the mixture.

Cream of tartar, tartaric acid and glucose are other ingredients used; these all help to avoid crystallisation. Naturally glucose imparts a sweet taste and liquid glucose also gives additional gloss and makes the mixture more pliable.

Where to buy ingredients

Milk and plain chocolate is obtainable from confectioners; the more specialised chocolate is sold by high class grocers and supermarkets. There are also some ready-made mixes on sale to use as fillings for chocolates. Most of the other ingredients for sweet-making are sold in grocers; you may have to order liquid glucose from a chemist.

EQUIPMENT

It is important to choose the right equipment when making chocolates or sweets as this will enable you to prepare professional looking and delicious confectionery. Some of the equipment required and listed below may well be part of your existing kitchenware, but other utensils, such as shaped moulds and dipping spoons or forks are produced especially for making confectionery. You will find these in cookshops carrying a good range of specialist utensils.

Here are the items you will use:

Boxes: to pack the confectionery in or other attractive containers (see page 74).

Brushes: you will need a fine brush, like a paintbrush, for coating moulds with a thin layer of melted chocolate. A good pastry brush is invaluable when boiling the mixture for fudge, toffee and similar sweets. Stand the brush in a bowl of cold water near the cooker and frequently brush down the inner sides of the pan. The sugar mixture rises in the pan during the cooking process and this action will prevent small amounts hardening and crystallising on the inside of the pan. Buy a good quality brush that will withstand heat. A second pastry brush is needed for brushing tins with melted butter or oil before filling. Wash the brushes in hot water to melt any sugar mixture on the bristles; rinse in cold water and dry well. Store carefully so the bristles remain a good shape.

Funnel: this will help when filling moulds with melted chocolate or hot fondant mixture. Clean in hot water and dry thoroughly.

Hammer: special confectionery hammers are necessary for breaking up hard sweets such as brittle toffee.

Heatproof basins or bowls: for melting chocolate over a pan of hot water; check that the basin is a good fit, so there is no possibility of it tilting or tipping over. Dry the damp outside of the basin so no steam or liquid can drip into the chocolate when it is being poured. If you plan to melt the chocolate in a microwave cooker or ordinary oven, as described on page 16, check that the utensils are suitable for this purpose.

Kitchen scissors: for cutting up certain sweets, such as jellies or marshmallows. Wash and dry straight after use.

Marble slab: this is used when kneading (often called 'working') certain sweet mixtures. You may be able to obtain one from a secondhand dealer or specialist shop, otherwise use a laminated board (this is better than a wooden one).

An Easter Egg (page 37)

Moulds: buy these gradually as you decide upon your particular requirements. Look around the house and see if you have any small containers in plastic or metal that would serve for making interesting shapes of melted chocolate or for creating homemade chocolates. Moulds are available in small rubber shapes, sold in sets (called 'mats'). These are primarily for fondant; as they are pliable it is easy to remove the firm fondant sweets from the moulds. Small plastic moulds enable you to shape chocolates, or you can buy larger shapes like Easter egg moulds. Metal moulds are also available, but are more expensive than the plastic ones and not as readily available. You can line small paper cases with melted chocolate, so these become a mould (see page 26). Wash rubber moulds in warm, but not hot, water and dry well. Store carefully so the flat mat does not lose its shape. Plastic moulds should never be put near dry heat; these should be washed in hand hot water, dried and stored carefully. Metal moulds must be washed in very hot water; make sure they are completely dry before putting away.

Saucepan: choose a strong pan with a flat base. In many recipes you will be heating the mixture to a very high temperature and this could burn in a thin pan or one with an uneven base. A saucepan with a large diameter and good depth will allow you to cook the sweet mixture fairly quickly without fear of it boiling over. A double saucepan can be used instead of a basin standing over a pan of hot water to melt chocolate. Saucepans can be difficult to clean unless you fill them with cold water immediately after use; heat the water until the sugar mixture left in the pan melts then tip this out and wash the pan as usual.

Scraper: although an ordinary palette knife can be used to pick up the sugar mixture from a slab or board when it is being handled, you will find the correct type of spatula or scraper more efficient; this is exceptionally pliable and yet strong.

Spoons: choose a wooden spoon or spatula for stirring, preferably one with a long handle that keeps your hand well away from the very hot mixture in the saucepan. You will also need a dipping spoon or fine dipping fork; this is to hold the sweet as it is being dipped and coated with either melted chocolate or a liquid fondant. As a substitute you could insert a fine metal or wooden skewer into the filling and dip it into the liquid coating, but a skewer does not support the filling in the same way as a spoon or fork. Wash wooden spoons or spatulas in warm water as soon as possible after use, before the sugar mixture has a chance to harden on them, and dry thoroughly. Clean metal dipping forks or spoons in very hot water.

Sweet cases: most sweets and chocolates look more attractive when placed in paper petits fours cases.

Sugar thermometer: while it is possible to gauge the temperature of some sweet mixtures without a thermometer, if you plan to do a lot of sweet-making then a sugar thermometer is virtually essential. Check before buying that it includes low temperatures, as these are necessary for tempering chocolate. Never remove the sugar thermometer from a very hot mixture to a cold or damp surface, but place it carefully on a cloth or wooden surface. When cold, clean gently in warm water, dry and store in a safe place.

Tins: flat metal Swiss roll tins are useful when leaving sweets to harden or set. You need slightly deeper tins in which to pour fudge, toffee and similar mixtures. Choose good quality ones, for thin tins could buckle when in contact with very hot mixtures. Wipe or wash as usual and dry thoroughly before putting away.

Waxed paper: this is an excellent base for chocolate work and also invaluable for wrapping sweets.

Wire cooling tray: this can be used to support various sweets and chocolates as they set; a fine meshed one is better for small sweets.

Wrapping paper: see page 74 for ideas on wrapping sweets and chocolates.

MELTING CHOCOLATE

The care with which chocolate is melted is of prime importance. If the chocolate is overheated it becomes scorched and is then no longer suitable for sweet-making. The chocolate should be heated only until it forms a smooth soft consistency that will coat fillings or moulds evenly.

There are several ways in which chocolate can be melted – but in a heatproof basin over hot water is the best way for beginners, as it is then easier to control and check the progress of melting. It is certainly the best method when tempering the chocolate for dipping (below).

Whichever method of melting is selected, it is important that the fillings for the chocolates are prepared and that any moulds or other equipment required are ready *before* the melting begins. This means that the chocolate can be used the moment it has reached the correct stage.

Melting over Hot Water

Prepare the chocolate by grating, breaking or cutting it into small pieces, or use chocolate drops or pieces. Put into a heatproof and absolutely dry basin or into the top of a double saucepan (often called a double boiler). Pour water into the pan underneath, making sure there is not too much, for the water must not touch the base of the basin or top part of the double saucepan. Heat the water, checking carefully that it does not boil. The ideal temperature of the water should be approximately 82 C/180 F i.e. hotter than your hands

could bear but below boiling point. Place the chocolate in its container over the hot water and leave until it just *begins* to melt. Remove from the heat – remember that the melting process will continue for a while due to the warmth of the container. If you are using chocolate couverture, bitter chocolate or chocolate menier, you will find it liquefies more readily than ordinary plain or milk chocolate which hold their shape longer and only liquefy and become smooth when stirred.

If melting chocolate to use for simple sweets, cut-outs or decoration, then this process, if carefully followed, is quite satisfactory. However, when making chocolates or filling large moulds you achieve a far better result if you check the melting point with a sugar thermometer. As the chocolate melts turn the thermometer gently in the chocolate, both to blend it and to ascertain the true heat, then read the setting.

The melting temperature varies very slightly with the make of chocolate, and this is given in detail opposite. After melting the chocolate, the next stage is to temper it. This term is used to denote the fact that the melted chocolate is cooled then reheated, but to a lower temperature than for the initial melting. The reasons for tempering, and the temperature to which the chocolate is reheated, are given opposite.

Melting in a Microwave Cooker

A microwave cooker provides a simple way of melting chocolate but it must be stressed that, if excess heat is used, it is possible to overheat and therefore scorch the chocolate.

Prepare the chocolate; put it into a heatproof dry bowl. If the cooker has variable heat it is wise to use a low setting, such as Defrost. As a rough guide, 100 g/4 oz plain block chocolate (broken into small squares) takes 4 minutes on Defrost setting in a cooker with a 600 watt output. Stir the chocolate at regular intervals. You cannot use an ordinary sugar thermometer in a microwave cooker.

Melting over Direct Heat

Choose a very strong saucepan; make sure it is quite dry inside. Prepare the chocolate and put into the saucepan. Set the heat on the hot-plate or gas burner to the lowest possible. Place the saucepan over the heat and stir the chocolate constantly until it starts to melt. Remove from the heat and continue stirring. The chocolate can be tested with a thermometer (see above).

Melting in the Oven

This is a method that needs the utmost care, for it is very easy to place the container and chocolate into the oven and then forget them. It must be stressed that the oven heat should be switched off and the heat retained in the oven must have dropped to a very low temperature. Prepare the chocolate, place in a dry ovenproof basin, put into the oven and leave until *nearly melted*; inspect the chocolate frequently. Bring out of the oven and stir until evenly melted. Most sugar thermometers cannot be placed in an oven.

TEMPERING CHOCOLATE

Tempering chocolate produces better results when making more elaborate chocolate confectionery. When chocolate is melted the fats in the cocoa butter melt and become well distributed. When the chocolate is cooled and then reheated to a lower setting some of these fats remain in crystallised form and so help to prevent a 'bloom', i.e. cloudiness forming on the surface of the chocolate. Chocolate that has not been treated like this, i.e. tempered correctly, may fail to set and harden quickly, this can cause problems when trying to remove the chocolate shapes from moulds, especially with large moulds like Easter eggs.

The stages of tempering are as follows:
1. Melt the chocolate, as already described, until it reaches the correct melting temperature.
2. Cool the chocolate rapidly. The professional method is to tip the liquid chocolate on to a clean and well dried marble slab, then spread it out with a palette knife to cool. It is then gathered up, returned to the basin or top of the double pan in which it was first melted, and slowly reheated to the second setting. As it reheats stir thoroughly, but not too vigorously, for that can create unwanted air bubbles.

If you feel this method of cooling the melted chocolate is too difficult then try the alternative: pour away the hot water under the container of melted chocolate; fill this with cold water and stand the container over the cold water to cool, stirring well all the time. When cool reheat again gently to the second temperature.

Temperatures to follow:
Plain chocolate couverture (varies)
Melting temperature: 46-47 C/115-117 F
Second temperature: 31 C/88 F
Milk chocolate couverture
Melting temperature: 43 C/110 F
Second temperature: 29 C/84 F
Plain chocolate (varies)
Melting temperature: 53-54 C/128-130 F
Second temperature: 28 C/83 F
Milk chocolate
Melting temperature: 41 C/106 F
Second temperature: 26 C/79 F

Mixture of 50% plain and 50% milk chocolate
Melting temperature: 42 C/108 F
Second temperature: 27 C/81 F
Treat white chocolate as milk chocolate but check most carefully during melting; it overheats easily.

Decorations for Chocolates
Have decorations readily available before making the chocolates, for the coating sets very rapidly, and nuts, crystallised flower petals and sugar dragees need to be pressed on to the half-set chocolate. A simple decoration is made by swirling the half-set coating with a fine skewer or dipping fork to give an interesting effect. Glacé or royal icings could be used to pipe on chocolates, or use melted chocolate; in this case the chocolate coating must first be firmly set.

A selection of dipped and moulded chocolates

Filled & Dipped Chocolates

This chapter gives suggestions and recipes for homemade filled chocolates. Do not attempt to make the chocolate for coating the various fillings at home; it is not an easy process since it requires the correct room temperature and atmosphere as well as the right ingredients. Concentrate instead on preparing professional-looking and interesting chocolates. To coat the various centres choose chocolate couverture, or top quality plain or milk block chocolate.

DIPPED CHOCOLATES

First assemble all the ingredients required; the fondant centres should be made into neat shapes; fudge, marzipan or other fillings cut into even squares or oblongs, or formed into ovals or small balls. Do not make the fillings too large and place as close to the working area as possible. There should be the minimum delay between melting and tempering the chocolate and then dipping the centres. All decorations should also be prepared and placed ready nearby.

Gather all the equipment needed: a double saucepan, or basin over a pan of hot water, for melting the chocolate; a wooden spoon or spatula to stir the chocolate; a sugar thermometer to assess the temperature of the melted and then tempered chocolate; a marble slab, or laminated board; wire cooling trays or tins, covered with waxed paper or foil (this is not ideal since it may crease in handling); a dipping spoon or fork (a skewer could be used, but is less efficient – a fondue fork is a good alternative); a piping bag and nozzle, if you intend to pipe decorations. Prepare the chocolate for melting; this means grating hard chocolate couverture or blocks or cutting these into smaller pieces. Melt the chocolate until it reaches the temperature given on page 17; stir to ensure you have an even heat before the final reading. If you do not have a thermometer then you must stir with the spoon or spatula and make quite certain that the chocolate does not overheat. Remove the container from the heat and temper the chocolate as described on page 17. This stage obviously can be done if you have no thermometer, but it is harder to gauge the correct heat.

Dip the first centre in the chocolate and turn it around with the dipping spoon or fork. When satisfied that the centre is evenly coated, lift out of the chocolate and hold it above the container so that any surplus chocolate drops back. If coating jellied sweets, such as Turkish Delight, you must allow the chocolate to cool, so it is advisable to coat these towards the end of the process. Place the coated chocolate on the waxed paper and put the decoration in place (unless using a piped decoration, in which case you must first wait for the coating chocolate to set).

Continue like this until all the centres have been coated. It is advisable to coat the larger centres first, so that when you are becoming rather short of chocolate you can coat whole blanched almonds or other nuts. If the chocolate becomes too cold during the coating process then it must be gently reheated and retempered.

When the chocolates are properly set, wrap individually or put into small petits fours cases and pack in attractive containers.

A CHOCOLATE SELECTION

A box of chocolates is most interesting if it is filled with different centres perhaps even covered with different kinds of chocolate. You might have some coated with plain chocolate, some with milk chocolate and some with a half-and-half mixture. It is also possible to include some coated with white chocolate. The chocolates can be different shapes, according to their centres.

Amounts to use

It is not easy to give precise amounts of chocolate and fillings, for this will depend upon the size of the fillings and the thickness of the coating chocolate, really a matter of personal taste.

As a general guide though, 450 g/1 lb chocolate should coat about 60-70 fillings and give a moderately thick coating of chocolate.

For perfect results

Follow the advice given about carefully melting and then tempering chocolate (see pages 16 and 17).

Do not be impatient, chocolate dipping takes time, so plan to make a selection of chocolates on a day when you have time to spare and will not be hindered.

Make the centres one or two days ahead, so these have time to set or harden. You will find ideas for fillings on page 20 and for a Basic Fondant on page 21, with some more unusual and interesting chocolate centres on the following pages.

Chocolate is very much affected by the atmosphere around, so make sure there is no steam in the kitchen from cooking or washing. Choose a really dry day for making chocolates of any kind – steam from the surroundings or from humidity in the air can make the chocolate dull and less inclined to set. Draughts also affect chocolate adversely, so never work or leave the chocolates near an open window.

Store the finished chocolates in a cool dry place.

Dipped Cherries (overleaf)

Chocolate Centres

The most suitable centres for coating are:

Candy: as the recipes on page 60, the less sweet flavours are better.

Caramels: every kind.

Cherries: either glacé or maraschino.

Coconut Ice: take care it does not crumble when dipping into the hot chocolate.

Fondants: every kind.

Fudge: the less rich types are better.

Jellied Sweets: such as Turkish Delight. The chocolate for coating must be cool (although still in a liquid state) so it does not melt the mixture.

Marzipan: the mixture can be softened very slightly by adding a few drops of sherry or liqueur; this gives a more succulent filling. Any marzipan sweets could be used instead of plain marzipan.

Nougat: if dipping in chocolate it is better not to coat this in rice paper, but to pour the mixture into a lightly oiled tin to set.

Nuts: various kinds, either as individual nuts or clusters.

Toffees: choose the softer varieties such as Golden or Everton Toffee, rather than the hard brittles.

Truffles: choose those made with firmer mixture, e.g. containing cake crumbs, rather than the piped truffles.

MOULDED CHOCOLATES

If the chocolate casing is melted and tempered and then put into a mould, you can use a more liquid filling inside if you wish. The finished chocolates also have a more interesting and professional looking shape.

Make sure the moulds are absolutely clean and free from any moisture. Pour or spoon in enough liquid chocolate to come about one-third of the way up the mould. Carefully and evenly, using a paint brush, spread the chocolate and coat the sides *almost* to the top of the moulds. Never paint to the very top, or when the final covering of chocolate is put on you may find it difficult to remove the sweets from the moulds. Put the chocolate coated moulds into a cool place until the chocolate has hardened; this makes certain it is not disturbed when the filling is added.

Put in the filling; this should be formed into the right shape if it is a fairly firm textured fondant, fudge or toffee, or otherwise put into the mould when it is sufficiently soft to form into the same shape as the mould. If the filling is very soft you can leave the chocolates once again for the filling to harden. Cover with melted chocolate; again take care in spreading this, so that it does not come over the edge of the mould. Keep in a cool place – the refrigerator can be used if the weather is very warm – until the chocolates are quite firm. Carefully turn out of the moulds. The easiest way is to invert the moulds over waxed paper; if the chocolate coating is really cold they will come out easily.

LIQUEUR CHOCOLATES

The liqueur chocolates based on a soft fondant are described on page 23. Another base for liqueur flavours can be made from packet fondant icing (the type sold to coat cakes). Work in enough liqueur to give a good flavour, then soften the mixture with a little cream if desired. Nowadays a packet base is sold by some cookshops specialising in equipment for homemade confectionery. Add the liqueur and other ingredients as directed.

Commercially made liqueur chocolates often have a liquid syrup liqueur mixture inside. This is only suitable if making moulded chocolates (see above and under Colettes on page 26). The recipe for the syrup is on page 26.

BASIC FONDANT FILLING

Fondant makes a delicious and very versatile filling for chocolate, as well as a good sweet on its own. The ideal fondant is firm on the outside but soft in the centre. There is a recipe for Uncooked Fondant on page 71 and this basic fondant can be flavoured and adapted in many ways.

450 g/1 lb granulated sugar
225 ml/7½ fl oz water
40 g/1½ oz glucose

Put the sugar and water into a strong saucepan, stir over a moderate heat until the sugar has dissolved, then add the glucose. Boil rapidly until the mixture reaches 'soft ball' stage or 115-118 C/240-245 F. The higher temperature produces a slightly firmer mixture than the usual soft ball; this is probably more suitable when making fondant as a separate sweet; a soft fondant mixture makes a better filling for chocolates. The fondant can be made softer still with various additions, see variations.

Do not beat the fondant in the pan, for this could make it granular, but allow it to cool and stiffen very

Piping on Chocolates (page 25)

slightly. Then sprinkle a little warm water on a slab and turn the fondant out of the pan; allow to stand for a few minutes more to set and cool slightly.

Work the fondant with a spatula or palette knife until it becomes very white and firm in texture. It is at this stage that small portions of the fondant can be removed to flavour and colour in various ways. Obviously if you want all the fondant flavoured in the same way you can add this to the mixture when first boiling it.

If you do not want to use the fondant at once then wrap it and store in a cool place.

To reheat fondant: take off the required amount, put into the top of a double saucepan or into a basin over a pan of boiling water. Heat until melted then use as required.

Variations
Use 300 ml/½ pint water and 20 g/¾ oz glucose to the 450 g/1 lb sugar; allow the mixture to boil until it reaches 114 C/238 F. This gives a slightly softer fondant. The same texture can be obtained by omitting the glucose in the basic recipe and using instead 2 level tablespoons golden syrup (measure the syrup carefully).

Flavoured Fondants

The following sweet or chocolate centres can be made by adding flavouring to either the Uncooked Fondant on page 71 or the Basic Fondant above.

Coffee Fondant: 2-3 teaspoons instant coffee powder to either of the recipes. You can substitute strong black coffee for the water in the cooked fondant.

Liqueur Coffee Fondant: Work a little Tia Maria or other coffee-flavoured liqueur into either of the fondants when handling; it will then give the soft texture correct for liqueur chocolates. Coarsely chopped walnuts or hazelnuts can be added to the mixture and the chocolates could be decorated with coffee beans (these can be chocolate coated) or with nuts.

Creamy Fondant: Work a little double cream into either of the uncooked or cooked fondant recipes; this can be the basis for other flavours and additions such as chopped nuts. It makes a particularly good filling for a plain chocolate coating.

Chocolate Fondant: Add a little melted chocolate to either of the fondant recipes plus a small amount of brandy or Curaçao. A little cream can also be added to give a really soft filling for chocolates. If you use melted milk chocolate in the filling and plain chocolate for coating you have a good variation of colour and flavour.

Ginger Fondant: Flavour the fondant with ground ginger, then wrap this around small pieces of preserved or crystallised ginger to make an interesting sweet or chocolate centre. The coated chocolates could be decorated with small pieces of crystallised ginger.

Honey Fondant: Blend a little honey into the completed fondant to make a soft sweet filling that is particularly good as a centre for plain or even bitter chocolate. Chopped nuts blend well with this, especially chopped Brazil or pecan nuts.

Lemon Fondant: Either flavour the fondant with a little lemon essence or add ½-1 teaspoon finely grated lemon rind to the mixture. In the cooked fondant the rind can be added in a more subtle way: use loaf instead of granulated sugar and rub the sugar lumps over lemons before cooking; in this way you absorb all the lemon flavour without having any lemon rind. Lemon juice could be used instead of some of the water in the cooked fondant recipe.

An interesting lemon filling, which is particularly suitable for the Moulded Chocolates on page 20, is to put a little creamy or lemon flavoured fondant into the chocolate casing, then add a small amount of lemon curd, top with more fondant and finally cover with chocolate. You could use this fondant and curd mixture for dipping in chocolate, provided the lemon curd is well enclosed in fondant.

Chocolate Nut Clusters (page 73), Chocolate Rum Truffles (page 28) and Chocolate Leaves (page 37)

Orange Fondant: Use orange rind and/or juice, or some Curaçao instead of the lemon flavourings suggested above. You could use a very little orange marmalade or orange curd in the centre of the chocolate mixture.

Peppermint Creams (illustrated on page 27): Flavour either the uncooked or cooked fondant with peppermint essence or oil of peppermint. A little double cream can be added but the mixture must be sufficiently firm to roll out to 5 mm/¼ inch thickness on a board lightly dusted with sifted icing sugar. Cut into 2·5-cm/1-in rounds; allow to harden. These can be fully dipped in melted chocolate, or just half coated. Crème de menthe and a few drops of pale green colouring can be used for a different version and some peppermint creams can be decorated with crystallised violets.

Peppermint Cream Logs (illustrated on page 32): Tint the fondant mixture green and flavour with peppermint essence or oil of peppermint. Break into small pieces and roll into log shapes, dusting your fingers and the board lightly with icing sugar. Dip in melted chocolate to coat one end only.

Raspberry or Strawberry Fondant: Work a little raspberry or strawberry essence and colouring into either the cooked or uncooked fondant – never make fondant sweets too bright in colour. Delicious chocolate centres can be made by half filling chocolate moulds with creamy raspberry or strawberry flavoured fondant, then adding whole fruit from raspberry or strawberry jam or a little liqueur. Top with more flavoured fondant and then cover with chocolate.

Moulded Fondants

Both cooked and uncooked fondants can be used for moulding, but the cooked fondant is better because it can be made softer. Simply pour the hot fondant into moulds and leave to set. If using uncooked fondant you should make this fairly soft, then press it into the moulds and leave until firm. You can of course mould fondant with your fingers; dust these first with sifted icing sugar. Moulded fondants can then be dipped in chocolate to make interesting and unusual shapes.

More Chocolate Fillings

Praline is one of the most popular fillings for chocolates. It blends with other mixtures too, as shown in the recipes below.

Praline Chocolates

Put 150 ml/¼ pint water and 225 g/8 oz granulated sugar into a strong saucepan; stir until the sugar has dissolved then boil the mixture, without stirring, until it becomes a golden brown caramel. Add a further 225 g/8 oz sugar, 50 g/2 oz unsalted butter and a little vanilla essence. Stir well until the second batch of sugar has dissolved then allow the mixture to boil until it reaches the 'soft ball' stage, or 115 C/240 F. Flavour the mixture by adding up to 225 g/8 oz chopped

blanched almonds, walnuts or pecan nuts, or use a mixture of finely chopped nuts. Pour the hot mixture into a greased 20-cm/8-in square tin and allow to set. Cut into neat squares. Dip in melted chocolate or use as a filling for Colettes (see page 26).

Chocolate Pralines

Follow the directions above and add 100 g/4 oz grated plain chocolate with the nuts. Coat in melted milk chocolate to give a variation in flavour.

Coconut Chocolate Pralines

Add 100 g/4 oz finely shredded or grated fresh or desiccated coconut to the mixture, together with 100 g/4 oz grated chocolate, instead of the chopped nuts. Coat in melted chocolate as for the basic recipe. In both this recipe and the one above it is better to allow the praline mixture to reach only 114 C/238 F. Top the coated chocolates with a little grated or dried coconut; press this into the soft chocolate coating before it is set.

Chambery Praline Chocolates

Allow any of the mixtures given above to set in a large tin, giving a thinner layer than usual; when firm cut into squares and coat with thin Almond Paste (see page 70). Dip in melted chocolate and top with whole almonds.

Pistachio Almond Chocolates

Blanch pistachio nuts in boiling water for 1 minute. Remove skins and dry the nuts, chop fairly finely and blend with Almond Paste (see page 70). Either roll the mixture into balls or cut into neat squares or oblong shapes. Coat in melted chocolate. Dip a few blanched and chopped pistachio nuts into a little more melted chocolate and spoon a very small amount on top of each chocolate to give an interesting topping.

Praline Date Chocolates

Select very good quality dates; remove the stones and fill the cavities with small portions of praline, as the basic recipe. Coat the dates with melted chocolate. Fresh rather than dried dates could be used, but these chocolates must not be stored for longer than a few days.

Almond Date Chocolates

Follow the recipe above, but fill the cavities in the dates with Almond Paste (see page 70). This could be blended with a few chopped almonds or a little sweet sherry. Coat the dates with melted chocolate and top with whole almonds.

Two-Layer Chocolates

Make a fudge recipe but pour the mixture into a large shallow tin, so that you have a thinner layer. Make some praline or choose a flavoured toffee that will blend with the flavour of the fudge you have made. Either allow this to set in another tin, or cool as much as possible and then pour it over the fudge to set. Cut the double layer sweet into squares or cut squares of fudge and squares of the other sweet and put these together. Coat in melted chocolate.

The idea of blending two different kinds of filling can be used for Colettes (see page 26) or any small moulded chocolates. Make the chocolate shell; allow this to harden. Half fill the chocolate shell with one layer of sweet. Allow time for this to set if necessary, then top up the mould with the second kind of sweet. When this is firm finally top with melted chocolate.

Fruit Balls

Melt 175 g/6 oz plain chocolate, blend with 100 g/4 oz chopped nuts, 100 g/4 oz minced or chopped dried apricots and 100 g/4 oz seedless raisins. Put small heaps on to waxed paper on a flat surface and allow to set. Coat in melted chocolate.

Other fruits could be coated in the same way.

Colettes (overleaf)

PIPING ON CHOCOLATES

After fillings have been dipped in chocolate you can frequently make an extra swirl in the chocolate on the top. A dipping fork or even an ordinary fork is better for this than a dipping spoon as it gives a more interesting design.

It is quite easy to decorate your chocolates with piping. You can use any leftover melted chocolate, or melt a little extra. You could make contrasting colours by piping white or milk chocolate on top of dark plain chocolate or vice versa.

The most useful shape of nozzle for piping is a No. 1 writing pipe. Insert this into a greaseproof paper bag, as though preparing to ice a cake. Make quite certain that the coating on the chocolates is firm before attempting to pipe on them. Check that the melted chocolate for piping has a steady, flowing consistency. If too liquid it will pour rapidly through the nozzle; if too stiff it will be difficult to pipe.

Pipe the required design on gently, i.e. parallel lines, small dots or swirls or even a letter, for example 'F' to indicate fondant filling.

A small rose pipe is also suitable for piping chocolate; this is particularly successful on Easter eggs.

Make quite sure the piping is dry before packing the chocolates. If you have piped a fairly elaborate design it is better not to wrap these chocolates, but to place them in individual cases.

More Elaborate Piping

The photograph on page 21 shows chocolates with a raised design in piping. To make this, first pipe the design with a fine writing pipe, as suggested above. Allow this to cool, then fill the piping bag with more melted chocolate of the same type, or use a different type. Pipe on top of the original design, so making it stand high above the chocolate coating.

When planning a design on Easter Eggs, or other large moulds, first work out the design on paper. Pipe the design in fine piping, as suggested above, then build on this. You can also use royal icing for piping on chocolate; the recipe for this is the same as for Uncooked Fondant (see page 71).

COLETTES
Illustrated on page 24

This name is given to chocolates that are moulded in small paper confectionery or petits fours cases. The fillings for Colettes can be similar to those for most chocolates, although as the shape is firm and set within a case you can choose fairly fragile or liquid fillings if you wish.

Some of the most popular fillings are soft fondant, praline and marzipan – flavour and soften this with a little sherry, or add finely chopped nuts for an interesting texture. The photograph on page 24 shows a soft pink fondant being spooned over glacé cherries in the chocolate case. Another filling could be a liqueur syrup, see below.

Liqueur Syrup: put 450 g/1 lb sugar and 175 ml/6 fl oz water into a strong saucepan, stir until the sugar has dissolved then boil the mixture until it reaches 106 C/223 F, just below the 'thread' stage. Keep the sides of the pan well brushed with cold water to prevent the sugar mixture crystallising. When the syrup reaches the correct temperature, cool slightly then add 4 tablespoons of your favourite liqueur. You could divide the sugar syrup between small containers and add a different liqueur to each batch. Use as a filling for moulded chocolates or Colettes.

To make Colettes
Melt and temper the chocolate (see pages 16 and 17). Have the small paper cases ready. As these are fairly fragile it helps to layer several together to support the case being coated. If you have tiny moulds or cocktail sized patty tins you can place the paper cases inside these.

Brush the melted chocolate quite thickly over the base and up the sides of the cases; do not allow the coating to come over the top edge of the cases, or you will find it difficult to remove the set Colettes. Put the chocolate coated cases into a cool place for a short time to set. Add the filling; if this has to harden leave the Colettes once again. Finally spoon or brush enough melted chocolate over the top to enclose the filling. Press on any decoration, such as crystallised rose or violet petals, or add a swirl of chocolate. If using a piped decoration allow the top layer to set first. Carefully remove the paper cases when the Colettes are completely set.

CHOCOLATE FRUITS
Illustrated on page 29

The combination of fruit and chocolate is very pleasant and many fruits lend themselves to being dipped in chocolate. These are delicious to serve as petits fours with after dinner coffee for they are both sweet and refreshing.

Naturally, if you coat dried fruit such as dates or raisins, portions of crystallised fruit or preserved fruit such as maraschino cherries, these will all keep as if using any other chocolate filling, but when coating fresh fruit it is advisable to keep these only one or two days. You could prepare them early in the morning for an evening party.

While plain or milk chocolate could be used to coat the fruits, white chocolate is a good choice. Follow directions for melting this on page 16, but remember that white chocolate needs a shorter melting time and a lower melting temperature. You may feel it is not worthwhile tempering the chocolate for something that will be eaten and enjoyed so soon after preparation, but if you do temper it you must watch the temperature carefully and follow the instructions for using milk chocolate (see pages 13 and 17).

The most suitable fruits for coating are fresh or maraschino cherries; grapes (seedless if possible); quartered fresh apricots or figs; pieces of pineapple or ripe pear; segments of seedless tangerines (such as clementines) and whole strawberries.

Prepare the fruit: stone cherries; deseed grapes if necessary, these look attractive in pairs; cut larger fruits into portions; pull away all pith from clementines. Do not hull the strawberries as the green stalks look so attractive. Allow the fruit to drain on a piece of absorbent kitchen paper and then blot as dry as possible with the paper.

A dipping spoon is better than a fork for these sweets as it will not pierce the fruit and allow any juice to flow; the drier the outside of the fruit the better the coating will adhere. Dip each portion of fruit in the melted chocolate, half coating or fully coating as you prefer, and then place on waxed paper over a wire sieve or tin. Allow to set and put into small paper cases. Store in a cool place.

To give a very light coating, brush the fruit with melted chocolate instead of dipping it; this allows the colour of the fruits to be seen through the chocolate.

Uncooked Coconut Ice (page 72), Fudge (page 54), Apple Squares (page 67), Stuffed Dates, Cherries and Walnuts (page 71), Harlequin Shapes (page 71) and Peppermint Creams (page 23)

Truffles

As well as being delicious and often unusual, truffles are ideal to offer with coffee at the end of a special meal. If using as a filling for chocolate, omit the coating given in the various recipes, though normally this is essential to cover the soft and delicate mixtures.

Although the recipes vary considerably, the basic method is similar. Press the ingredients together as firmly as possible; if the truffle mixture seems rather soft, chill it well before forming into balls. The size varies – you may prefer them a little larger than given. The suggested number made is based upon each truffle weighing about 7 g/¼ oz before coating.

To coat the truffles, put the icing sugar, or other ingredients, on to a flat dish and gently turn the small balls in this. If preferred, put the coating into a greaseproof or polythene bag, drop in the small balls and shake gently until thickly coated. The amount of coating given is often a generous one but this is necessary.

A richer truffle mixture, and a different method, is used in the recipe for Dutch Truffles. These are piped and need no coating, but should be placed in individual petits fours cases.

CHOCOLATE RUM TRUFFLES
Illustrated on page 22

100 g/4 oz plain chocolate
3 tablespoons sweetened condensed milk
2 teaspoons rum
75 g/3 oz fine plain cake crumbs
To Coat:
25 g/1 oz icing sugar, sifted
25 g/1 oz cocoa powder or drinking chocolate

Melt the chocolate in a heatproof basin over a pan of very hot, but not boiling, water. Add the condensed milk and rum and allow to cool until the mixture becomes slightly sticky. Put in the cake crumbs; mix thoroughly. Form into approximately 30 small balls. Blend the icing sugar with the cocoa or chocolate powder and use to coat the truffles.

Variations
Use full-cream dried milk powder instead of cake crumbs. Chop 25 g/1 oz glacé cherries and add to the mixture with the crumbs.

Rum and Almond Truffles: use 75 g/3 oz marzipan instead of cake crumbs. Work the rum into the marzipan then blend with the melted chocolate and only 1½ tablespoons condensed milk.

The rum could be omitted and the mixture flavoured with a few drops of almond essence and 2 teaspoons sweet sherry.

Honey Almond Truffles: omit the condensed milk in the recipe, add instead 2 tablespoons thick honey together with 50 g/2 oz very finely chopped blanched almonds. The truffles can be coated as in the recipe above, or use chocolate vermicelli or toasted chopped blanched almonds.

Chocolate Fruits (page 26)

DUTCH TRUFFLES
Illustrated opposite

These truffles are made by piping a soft chocolate mixture into an attractive shape around hazelnuts. The mixture needs to be chilled in the refrigerator or even placed in the freezer for a short time until it is firm enough to handle.

225 g/8 oz plain chocolate
75 g/3 oz unsalted butter
25 g/1 oz icing sugar, sifted
2 tablespoons whipped double cream
few drops vanilla essence
For the Centres:
about 24 blanched hazelnuts

Grate the chocolate or break into small pieces. Melt by one of the methods given on page 16. Cool but do not allow to harden again. Cream the butter; add the sugar and blend in the cooled chocolate. When the mixture is quite cold, add the whipped cream and essence. Chill to give a piping consistency that will hold a good shape.

Put a rose-shaped nozzle into a piping bag. Fill with the truffle mixture and pipe small flat rounds on to waxed paper on a flat surface. Place the hazelnuts in the centre of these and pipe the truffle mixture around and over the nuts. Chill well.

Variations

Melt a little extra plain chocolate, spread this on to a flat surface and allow to set. Cut the chocolate into small rounds using a pastry or cocktail cutter. Put the truffle mixture into a piping bag and press out a small amount of the mixture in the centre of each chocolate round. Press the hazelnut in position. Pipe the rest of the truffle mixture over the nut and chill well.

Make chocolate cases as for Colettes, and fill with the piped truffle mixture.

Flavour the truffle mixture with 1 tablespoon rum, or use portions of walnuts, pecan nuts or cashew nuts, or flavoured fondant, instead of the hazelnuts.

ANGOSTURA TRUFFLES

175 g/6 oz plain chocolate
½-¾ teaspoon Angostura Bitters
3 egg yolks
75 g/3 oz butter
75 g/3 oz icing sugar, sifted
To Coat:
25 g/1 oz cocoa powder, sifted
25 g/1 oz desiccated coconut
25 g/1 oz icing sugar, sifted
chocolate buttons (optional)

Break the chocolate into pieces. Melt in a heatproof basin over a pan of very hot, but not boiling, water and cool slightly. Add the Angostura Bitters and egg yolks to the melted chocolate and mix well. Place back over hot water and whisk until thick and creamy. Cream the butter and icing sugar until soft, then gradually blend in the chocolate mixture. Chill well then form into 40 small balls.

Blend the cocoa powder, coconut and icing sugar and use to coat the balls. They are very soft, so must be well coated. Place in petits fours cases and press a chocolate button in the top of each one, if liked.

APRICOT CHOCOLATE TRUFFLES

100 g/4 oz plain chocolate
100 g/4 oz dried apricots
40 g/1 ½ oz ground almonds
1 tablespoon sieved apricot jam
25 g/1 oz icing sugar, sifted
½ tablespoon apricot brandy
To Coat:
25 g/1 oz chocolate vermicelli

Melt the chocolate in a heatproof basin over a pan of very hot, but not boiling, water. Mince the apricots or put into a food processor and work to a smooth purée. Mix all the ingredients together. Chill well, form into about 36 small balls and coat in the chocolate vermicelli.

Dutch Truffles (opposite)

CHERRY TRUFFLES

50 g/2 oz icing sugar, sifted
50 g/2 oz cocoa or drinking chocolate powder, sifted
100 g/4 oz fine plain cake crumbs
4 tablespoons sieved apricot jam
2 teaspoons apricot brandy
24 glacé cherries

Put half the icing sugar and half the cocoa or chocolate powder into a bowl, add the cake crumbs, apricot jam and brandy and mix well. Divide into 24 portions and mould around the cherries.

Mix the remaining icing sugar and cocoa or chocolate powder together and use to coat the truffles.

Note The cocoa powder makes a very strongly flavoured mixture.

Variation
Coat in chocolate vermicelli.

CREAM TRUFFLES

50 g/2 oz mixed dried fruit
4 tablespoons double cream
few drops vanilla essence
75 g/3 oz icing sugar, sifted
40 g/1 ½ oz drinking chocolate powder
75 g/3 oz fine plain cake or sweet
plain biscuit crumbs
To Coat:
50 g/2 oz chocolate vermicelli or
plain chocolate, finely grated

Chop the dried fruit into smaller pieces with kitchen scissors. Whip the cream until just stiff then blend with the vanilla essence, icing sugar, chopped fruit, chocolate powder and crumbs. Form into about 40 small balls and roll in the chocolate vermicelli or grated chocolate. Chill well.

APRICOT COCONUT TRUFFLES

Illustrated on page 35

100 g/4 oz dried apricots
50 g/2 oz walnuts or other nuts
50 g/2 oz desiccated coconut
25 g/1 oz icing sugar, sifted
grated rind of 1 orange
apricot brandy or orange juice
(see method)
To Coat:
25 g/1 oz desiccated coconut

Mince the apricots and nuts or put into a food processor and work until finely chopped. Add the coconut, sugar, orange rind and just sufficient brandy or juice to bind. Form into 30-36 small balls and coat in the coconut.

MIXED FRUIT TRUFFLES

75 g/3 oz dried apricots
50 g/2 oz stoned dates
75 g/3 oz dried figs
75 g/3 oz raisins
50 g/2 oz mixed nuts
50 g/2 oz mixed crystallised peel
50 g/2 oz desiccated coconut
To Coat:
50 g/2 oz desiccated coconut
25 g/1 oz icing sugar, sifted

Finely mince all the truffle ingredients, except the desiccated coconut, or put into a food processor and work to give a sticky purée. Add the coconut. Form into about 60 small balls, oblongs or finger shapes.

Blend the coconut for coating with the icing sugar and roll the balls in this mixture.

Variations

Omit the dried figs and use glacé cherries instead. The mixture can be flavoured with a very little rum or brandy.

A selection of truffles and Peppermint Cream Logs (page 23)

Shaping Chocolates

A variety of shapes can be created from chocolate, and there are many ways in which these can be produced.

Grated chocolate and chocolate curls come *from chocolate that has not been melted first. The chocolate should be as firm as possible; in hot weather chill the block for a short time.*

PIPED CHOCOLATE SHAPES

Many shapes can be produced by first piping the outline of the shape and then filling this in with chocolate if desired.

Draw the outlines of flowers, animals, little figures, letters or numbers, or any other shapes you want on to waxed paper. Place the waxed paper on a flat tin.

Fit a fine writing pipe into a greaseproof piping bag. Melt the chocolate and temper this if possible. Put the melted chocolate into the bag and carefully pipe around the outline of the shapes. You can then decide to fill in the shapes with more melted chocolate, or simply to leave an interesting chocolate outline. Allow the chocolate to harden then carefully remove from the waxed paper with a palette knife.

Store in a box and separate each layer with waxed paper so the shapes do not break .

SOLID CHOCOLATE SHAPES

You can make solid shapes with chocolate using small moulds. First polish the moulds with a soft cloth or soft paper. Melt and temper the chocolate as described on pages 16 and 17; this is very important to ensure that the chocolate sets properly and remains clear and bright in colour. You can use any type of chocolate for this purpose, either milk, white or plain.

Pour the chocolate in a steady stream into the mould or moulds; a funnel is ideal for this. Tap the moulds to make sure there are no air bubbles in the chocolate and allow to set in a cool dry place.

The chocolate shape will contract and be easily removed from the mould. Do not be too impatient though, the depth of chocolate means it may take several hours to harden; ideally make the shapes one day and leave them to the next until set. Decorate as wished and wrap in foil type paper.

Apricot Coconut Truffles with Chocolate Rum Truffles (page 33 and 28) and a selection of hand-made chocolates

CHOCOLATE MOULDS

These are not difficult to make; obviously you must first buy the metal or plastic moulds in which to set the various chocolate shapes. Plastic has an advantage in that you can see when these are evenly coated.

It is not difficult to remove the chocolate shell from the moulds if the chocolate has first been melted and tempered carefully (see pages 16 and 17). The chocolate contracts when it is set and after 3 to 4 hours should be ready to lift out. Scrape away any surplus chocolate from the rims of the moulds and gently ease out the chocolate shape.

Make quite certain there is no steam in the kitchen when you plan to make chocolate moulds; avoid draughts and choose a dry day with as little humidity as possible. Polishing moulds may sound unnecessary but this makes a great difference to the ease with which the chocolate shells can be taken out of the moulds.

Making Easter Eggs (opposite)

Grating Chocolate

Simple coatings for truffles or for sprinkling on top of chocolates are made by grating block chocolate or chocolate couverture. Use the finest side of the grater; it is easier to grate a fairly thick block of chocolate that will not break when handled. Sprinkle the grated chocolate on top of dipped chocolates or Colettes when the coating is almost, but not quite, hard. Press the grated chocolate gently against the chocolate surface with a flat-bladed knife.

By using a slightly coarser grater you will make a good decoration for gâteaux and desserts.

Making Chocolate Curls

One or two chocolate curls can be put on top of chocolates instead of grated chocolate. Naturally these curls must be very small for this purpose; larger curls make an excellent decoration on cakes and gâteaux.

A good vegetable peeler is ideal for making small curls; check that it is absolutely dry. Hold the block of chocolate upright in one hand then slowly scrape the vegetable peeler from the base towards the top of the block. The chocolate will form curls. Select the small curls for decorating chocolates; pack the larger curls carefully in a box and use these for cakes or desserts or to sprinkle on ice cream.

The following shapes are made with melted chocolate; follow one of the methods given on page 16. If you are making only a few decorations you may not feel it worthwhile tempering the chocolate. If, however, you are planning to produce a good batch of decorations then tempering, as described on page 17, will make certain the chocolate sets firmly and that the shapes will be easily produced.

Chocolate Caraque

The term 'caraque' is used to describe chocolate when formed into long curls.

To make chocolate caraque, melt the chocolate and temper it if possible. Spread the melted chocolate on to a marble slab or laminated board, to give a fairly thick layer of about 1-1·5 cm/½-¾ in. Allow the chocolate to set and become hard. Hold a sharp knife across it at an angle of 45° and slowly and carefully draw the knife towards you, to give curls.

Caraque could be used as a topping for large open chocolate moulds but its main value is as a topping on gâteaux.

Cut-out Chocolate Shapes

Melt the chocolate and temper this if possible. Spread the melted chocolate to give a thin layer on a marble slab or laminated board. If the surface is not absolutely perfect, i.e. in the case of a wooden board, then cover it with waxed paper and spread the chocolate over the paper. While the chocolate layer should be thin, remember that the thinner the chocolate the more brittle and fragile the shapes will be.

Leave until barely set then use miniature cocktail cutters to produce various shapes, e.g. hearts, diamonds, clubs, spades, rounds, tiny leaf shapes, bell shapes, triangles and squares. These can be served on their own or used for decoration. The surplus chocolate around the shapes should be gathered up; it can be melted later or used for other purposes.

Chocolate Leaves

While leaves can be produced by using leaf-shaped cutters, a more realistic effect is achieved if the chocolate is allowed to set on real leaves. Choose perfect leaves, those with a well-defined shape are the most effective; rose, geranium and violet leaves are particularly good. Make sure the leaves are dry and then coat the side of the leaf with the most definite veining; when the chocolate sets it will have the veining marks.

Melt the chocolate and temper it if possible. Either paint the liquid chocolate over the surface of the leaves or dip the underside of each leaf into the chocolate. Place the leaves with the chocolate coating upper-most. Allow to harden then carefully peel away the real leaves.

EASTER EGGS
Illustrated on page 38

It is not difficult to make Easter eggs at home. Use plain or milk chocolate, or you can achieve a very good flavour by melting together equal amounts of both.

It is essential to read the information on melting and tempering chocolate (see pages 16 and 17), for the chocolate will not harden well if the right processes have not been followed. The various stages involved in making your own eggs may seem complicated, but they are in fact very easy to follow.

Stage 1. Prepare the two oval-shaped moulds that will be joined together to form the completed egg. With a soft cloth or soft paper, carefully polish the inside of either plastic or metal moulds until they have a high gloss. Cover a flat tray or tin with waxed paper.

Stage 2. Melt and temper the chocolate until it reaches the correct temperatures as given on page 17.

Stage 3. Hold one mould in the palm of your hand to support it and spoon in enough melted chocolate to fill the mould to about one-third of its depth. Hold the edges of the mould with both hands and tip and turn it carefully until the sides are evenly coated with melted chocolate. If there is any surplus chocolate in the mould pour this back into the bowl or saucepan. If you find this is getting a little too firm replace over hot water as you work — but remember not to exceed the tempering temperature. Repeat this coating process with the second mould.

Stage 4. When coated turn each mould upside down (curved side uppermost) on the waxed paper. Leave for about 30 minutes or longer until the thin layer of chocolate is firm.

Stage 5. Slip a palette knife under each mould and lift away from the paper.

Stage 6. Check that the melted chocolate is at the right stage for re-coating the mould. If necessary heat gently.

Repeat Stage 3 with both moulds, so giving a second coating of chocolate. Invert each mould on to clean waxed paper and leave for 3 or 4 hours or even longer, until the chocolate coating is completely set and hard.

Stage 7. Scrape away any surplus chocolate from around the rims of the two moulds; do this slowly and carefully so you do not break the shells. You must however have even edges, so the two halves can be joined together and to make the shells easier to remove from the moulds. Melt a little more chocolate to join the halves together.

Stage 8. Insert the fingers of one hand into the first chocolate shape, while holding the mould firmly with the other hand. Gently lift the chocolate shell from the mould. Put upside down on waxed paper. Repeat with the second half of the egg.

Stage 9. Cut two squares of waxed paper, each large enough to cover the palm of your hand. This is important, for the less the egg shapes are touched with fingers the more perfect the chocolate surface will remain. Pick up the first chocolate shape with the waxed paper. Hold this carefully with the rim upper-most, spread or pipe a band of melted chocolate around the rim. Repeat with the second chocolate shell. Hold the second chocolate egg shape on the waxed paper and, gently but firmly, press this down on to the first shape, so the two edges fit together. Hold them gently together for several minutes if possible.

Stage 10. Secure with a band of waxed paper pinned around the egg and leave for several hours on waxed paper on a flat tin.

Stage 11. Remove the paper band and add any decorations to the egg. You can also pipe a band of chocolate around the join if desired.

The photograph above shows some of the ways in which Easter eggs can be decorated. You can make small flower shapes in royal icing (made as for Uncooked Fondant on page 71); pipe on to waxed paper or icing nails and leave these to set. Put a small blob of melted chocolate or icing on the egg and gently press these decorations into place.

You may like to make more elaborate decorations and use real spring flowers to decorate the egg. Allow the decorations to dry, then tie ribbon around the egg if desired. It is inadvisable however, to try and do too elaborate piping on the egg as it is fairly fragile and sudden pressure could make it break.

The eggs can be wrapped, but if very decorative it is better to leave them unwrapped.

If you are feeling ambitious you could even mould your own chocolate basket in which to stand that very special egg (illustrated on page 15).

A slightly different idea for Easter would be to use two chocolate eggs to make a Humpty Dumpty novelty cake, as shown in the photograph – this would certainly be popular with children.

Fondant Eggs
Pour soft fondant (see page 21) into heatproof egg cups and allow to set. Remove from the egg cups, dip into melted chocolate and leave to set on waxed paper. Spread melted chocolate around the rims of the halves and press carefully together. Allow to set.

Marzipan Eggs
Use Almond Paste (see page 70) instead of the fondant and proceed as above.

Miniature Easter Eggs
Mould fondant or marzipan into tiny egg shapes then coat in melted chocolate.

SWEETS AND CHOCOLATES FOR CHRISTMAS

There are many sweets that can be prepared for Christmas time. Fill boxes or pretty containers with assorted sweets and chocolates; these would sell well for charity and also make welcome presents.

Make cut-out shapes in chocolate to serve at the end of a special meal or to use as festive decorations on cakes and desserts.

Put wrapped chocolate coated animal shapes into children's stockings. You can of course make fondant shapes, as described above, and leave these plain without a chocolate coating.

Father Christmas shapes in chocolate would be extremely popular. If you do not possess the correct metal cutter, then you could draw the shape on thick card and cut around this with a sharp knife. Alternatively, pipe the outline and fill this in with melted chocolate.

It is possible to buy Father Christmas moulds and this more solid shape would be even more acceptable, see below.

Father Christmas

These make excellent Christmas presents. Buy moulds in the correct shape and carefully follow the stages for making Easter eggs. Wrap the shapes in coloured or clear cellophane paper when set.

Chocolate Animals

These will be popular at any time of the year. In order to make realistic animals you need two animal shaped shells, which are made and then joined together just like Easter eggs.

The photograph on page 38 shows an attractive Easter Rabbit. When the two chocolate moulds have been joined together and set, outline the ears and other features with royal icing (made as for Uncooked Fondant on page 71) or with melted white chocolate.

Fondant Chocolate Animals

These can be made in three ways:

Method 1 First pour the liquid fondant into the two moulds; allow to set. Remove from the moulds and dip in melted chocolate. Put the animal shapes flat side downwards on to waxed paper and leave to set. When firm spread the flat surfaces of the animals with a little melted chocolate and press together.

Method 2 Pour melted chocolate into the two moulds and turn until evenly coated. Allow to set then fill with liquid fondant; this should not be too hard. Leave until the fondant is firm then remove from the moulds. Spread melted chocolate over the rims and flat sides of the animals and press the two halves together.

Method 3 Mould animal shapes in fondant then coat with melted chocolate and allow to set. Decorate with piped eyes, noses and mouths.

Decorated Easter Eggs (previous page) and an Easter Rabbit

Toffees & Caramels

This chapter covers toffees of all kinds, including Everton Toffees, Golden Toffee and Honeycomb Toffee. There are also lots of ideas for flavouring toffee, for example Chocolate Toffee, Coconut Toffee, Peppermint Toffee and many more. Children love making toffee, but the mixture has to be cooked to a very high temperature, so an adult has to be in charge of the operation.

Following recipes for toffee, there is a selection of recipes for caramels. There is a considerable variety of ways in which caramels can be flavoured and by adjusting the heat to which the mixture is boiled, you can produce soft, medium, hard or very hard caramels.

TOFFEES

These are possibly the greatest favourites of all, and, fortunately, toffee is comparatively simple to make. Some toffees do become sticky with storage however so avoid making large amounts at one time.

Toffee recipes vary appreciably. In most recipes butter, sugar and water are boiled to a high temperature. In other recipes golden syrup or treacle are added. The mixture should be stirred as little as possible. The temperature to which toffee should be brought is a very high one, in most cases it is the 'hard crack' stage, i.e., 143·3 C/290 F. Because the mixture is boiled to such a high temperature, care should be taken that it does not overheat and burn or splash over the sides of the pan. Great care should also be taken when testing for the right temperature.

The toffee in one or two recipes is unsuitable for keeping, but this is clearly stated in the recipe. Most toffees should be individually wrapped in waxed paper before storing carefully in airtight tins or containers.

EVERTON TOFFEE I

A buttery toffee.

450 g/1 lb granulated or demerara sugar
100 g/4 oz butter
1 teaspoon lemon juice or white malt vinegar
150 ml/¼ pint water

Put the ingredients into a strong saucepan; stir over a moderate heat until the sugar has dissolved. Boil fairly briskly to the 'hard crack' stage or 143 C/290 F; stir as little as possible.

Grease a 20-cm/8-in square sandwich tin with a little butter; pour in the mixture. Allow to set lightly then mark into squares. Do not remove from the tin until cold. If preferred leave the toffee to set firmly as a slab then break into pieces. Wrap the individual pieces or slab in waxed paper.

Fruit Toffee and Russian Caramels (pages 43 and 47); Brazil Nut Toffee (page 43) and Toasted Coconut Caramels (page 47)

EVERTON TOFFEE 2

100 g/4 oz butter
225 g/8 oz golden syrup
225 g/8 oz demerara sugar

Put the butter into a strong saucepan and stir over a very low heat until melted. Add the syrup and sugar and stir well until dissolved. Boil fairly briskly to the 'hard crack' stage or 143 C/290 F; stir as little as possible.

Grease a 20-cm/8-in square sandwich tin with a little butter, pour in the mixture. Allow to set lightly then mark into squares. Do not remove from the tin until cold. If preferred leave the toffee to set firmly as a slab then break into pieces. Wrap the individual pieces or slab in waxed paper.

HONEYCOMB TOFFEE

Illustrated opposite

250 g/9 oz granulated sugar
40 g/1 ½ oz butter or margarine
3 tablespoons golden syrup
3 tablespoons water
6 drops white malt vinegar
1 ½ teaspoons bicarbonate of soda

Put the sugar, butter or margarine, syrup and water into a large strong saucepan. It is important to have a large pan because the mixture rises drastically in the pan when the bicarbonate of soda is added.

Stir over a moderate heat until the sugar has dissolved. Boil briskly until the mixture reaches 'hard crack' stage or 143 C/290 F. Stir in the vinegar and bicarbonate of soda.

Grease an 18-cm/7-in square sandwich tin with a little butter; pour in the mixture. Leave until set and cold then break into pieces. As the name suggests, this toffee has a honeycomb texture.

Note Measure the bicarbonate of soda carefully as the teaspoons must be level. It is advisable to make only a small quantity of this toffee at a time since it becomes very sticky if kept too long.

CHOCOLATE TOFFEE

350 g/12 oz granulated sugar
100 g/4 oz golden syrup
150 ml/¼ pint water
50 g/2 oz butter
175 g/6 oz plain chocolate

Put all the ingredients, except the chocolate, into a strong saucepan; stir over a moderate heat until dissolved. Boil steadily until the mixture reaches 'moderately hard crack' stage or 141 C/286 F. The chocolate will help to set the toffee so you can have a slightly lower boiling temperature.

Break the chocolate into small pieces, add to the pan and stir away from the heat until the chocolate has blended with the toffee mixture.

Grease a 23-cm/9-in square sandwich tin with a little butter; pour in the mixture. Allow to set lightly then mark into squares. Leave in the tin until cold then wrap in waxed paper.

Variations
Chocolate Orange Toffee: use orange juice instead of water in the recipe above; add 2 teaspoons finely grated orange rind.

175 g/6 oz plain chocolate can be added to Everton Toffee 1 (see page 40) or Golden Toffee (see opposite) just before the 'hard crack' stage. Everton Toffee 2 (see left) has a rather high percentage of golden syrup which would overpower the flavour of chocolate, if this were added.

GOLDEN TOFFEE

A good basic recipe.

450 g/1 lb demerara sugar
200 ml/7 fl oz water
40 g/1 ½ oz butter
2 tablespoons golden syrup
1 teaspoon brown or white malt vinegar

Put all the ingredients into a strong saucepan. Stir over a moderate heat until the sugar has dissolved. Boil fairly briskly to the 'hard crack' stage or 143 C/290 F; stir as little as possible.

Grease a 20-cm/8-in square sandwich tin with a little butter; pour in the mixture. Allow to set lightly then mark into squares. Do not remove from the tin until cold. If preferred leave the toffee to set firmly as a slab then break into pieces. Wrap the individual pieces or slab in waxed paper.

Making Honeycomb Toffee

Variations on Golden or Everton Toffees

Follow the recipe for Golden Toffee or one of the Everton Toffees and adapt as follows:

Almond Toffee: blanch up to 175 g/6 oz almonds. Chop coarsely and add to the mixture just before it reaches the 'hard crack' stage. The almonds can also be left whole and pressed on top of the toffee when it begins to set in the tin.

Brazil Nut Toffee (illustrated on page 41): chop 175 g/6 oz nuts coarsely and add to the mixture just before it reaches the 'hard crack' stage. Some can be halved and pressed on top of the toffee when it begins to set in the tin.

Coconut Toffee: add 100-175 g/4-6 oz desiccated coconut to the toffee mixture after it has come to the boil.

Fruit Toffee (illustrated on page 41): you can use all raisins or all sultanas or a mixture of dried fruits. If using large raisins, deseed them and cut into halves or quarters with kitchen scissors. Allow 100-175 g/4-6 oz fruit and add to the toffee just before it reaches 'hard crack' stage. If the fruit is inclined to be dry, put it in the mixture a little earlier; this gives it an opportunity to become more moist.

Peppermint Toffee: add up to 1 teaspoon peppermint essence or a few drops of oil of peppermint to the mixture when the sugar has dissolved. It is wise to be sparing with the quantity of flavouring at first, then add more later if required.

Rum Toffee: if using the Golden Toffee or Everton Toffee 1 recipe, omit 1-2 tablespoons water and substitute rum instead. In the Everton Toffee 2 recipe, add the rum to the other ingredients. Up to 1 teaspoon rum essence could be used instead of rum; do not reduce the water in the recipes.

Treacle or Molasses Toffee: substitute black treacle or molasses for the golden syrup in the Golden Toffee recipe.

CREAMY TREACLE TOFFEE

350 g/12 oz soft light brown sugar
50 g/2 oz butter
75 g/3 oz golden syrup
75 g/3 oz black treacle
6 tablespoons sweetened condensed milk
1½ teaspoons brown malt vinegar

Put all the ingredients into a strong saucepan and stir over a low heat until the sugar has dissolved. Boil steadily, stirring occasionally until the mixture reaches 'light crack' stage or 138 C/280 F. This is less hard than most toffees.

Oil a 23-cm/9-in square sandwich tin and pour in the mixture. Allow to set lightly then mark into squares. Leave in the tin until cold then wrap in waxed paper.

Variation

Creamy Toffee: the recipe above makes an excellent creamy toffee if the black treacle is omitted and a total of 175 g/6 oz golden syrup is used instead. 100 g/4 oz chopped nuts can be added.

PEANUT BUTTER TOFFEE

450 g/1 lb demerara sugar
200 ml/7 fl oz water
40 g/1½ oz butter
75 g/3 oz peanut butter
2 tablespoons golden syrup
1 teaspoon vinegar

Put the sugar, water and butter into a strong saucepan, stir over a low heat until the sugar has dissolved then add the remaining ingredients and blend thoroughly together. Boil to 'hard crack' stage or 143 C/290 F.

Grease a 20-cm/8-in square sandwich tin with a little butter and pour in the mixture. Allow to set lightly then mark into squares. Do not remove from the tin until cold. Wrap the individual pieces in waxed paper.

Barley Sugar Sticks and Edinburgh Rock (page 52), Peanut Brittle (page 50) and Butterscotch (page 48)

PULLED TAFFY

Taffy is generally considered to be the old-fashioned name for toffee, but the original taffy was frequently a pulled sweet, as in this recipe.

225 g/8 oz demerara sugar
175 g/6 oz golden syrup
100 g/4 oz butter
2 tablespoons warm water
2 teaspoons glucose

Put all the ingredients into a strong saucepan; stir over a low heat until the sugar has dissolved. Boil steadily until the mixture reaches 'light crack' stage, 129-131 C/265-268 F. Brush a slab or tin with a little melted butter or oil, pour the hot mixture on to the slab. When cool enough to handle, pull gently until you have made long strips of even thickness. Use just your fingertips to pull the sweet; if it sticks either dampen your fingers or dip them in cornflour.

Cut the taffy into neat pieces with kitchen scissors brushed with melted butter or oil, and wrap in waxed paper.

Variations

Black Treacle Taffy: use the same amount of sugar and water as above but substitute black treacle for the golden syrup. Omit the butter and glucose and add 1 teaspoon vinegar. Boil the mixture to the 'light crack' stage as above. Remove the pan from the heat, blend in 25 g/1 oz butter and ¼ teaspoon bicarbonate of soda. Mix thoroughly then proceed as above.

Peppermint Taffy: use the basic recipe and flavour this with a few drops of oil of peppermint or ½-1 teaspoon peppermint essence. Other essences, e.g. rum or almond, could also be used.

CARAMELS

Caramels are a very popular sweet; there is not only considerable variety in the way caramels can be flavoured, but, by adjusting the heat to which the mixture is boiled, you can produce soft, medium, hard or very hard caramels.

They are made by boiling liquid (water and milk or cream) with sugar; glucose and/or cream of tartar are added and some recipes contain butter. Careful attention to temperature is essential. If you intend to make caramels frequently you are well advised to buy a sugar thermometer, since the temperature to which the mixture has to boil is a little difficult for the beginner to ascertain. The mixture for a soft caramel should reach 'firm ball' stage or 121·1 C/250 F; for a moderately firm caramel allow to reach 'firmer ball' stage or 126·6 C/260 F; for a really firm hard caramel allow to reach 'very firm ball' stage or 129·4-132·2 C/265-270 F (also known as 'light crack' or 'soft crack').

Caramel is a sweet that must be stirred well to dissolve the sugar, then stirred from time to time as the mixture cooks. Make sure the saucepan is sufficiently large to facilitate cooking evenly and rapidly. The correct use of glucose or cream of tartar in the recipes prevents a tendency for the mixture to become gritty, but too much glucose will hinder the mixture from setting.

Caramels are quite difficult to cut. One can buy special caramel cutters but, providing the sweet is marked firmly when it is half set, it should not be difficult to cut when cold with a sharp knife. It is advisable to wrap each caramel in waxed paper to retain the correct texture. Caramels coated in chocolate do not need wrapping. Store in an airtight tin or box.

A caramel mixture is not suitable for storing and repeated reheating. If, however, a batch of caramels has become over-sticky due to exposure to the air, put them into a saucepan and stir continually until the mixture melts, then bring back to the temperature given in the original recipe.

CREAMY VANILLA CARAMELS

450 g/1 lb granulated sygar
150 ml/¼ pint milk
150 ml/¼ pint evaporated canned milk
or single cream
1 teaspoon vanilla essence
75 g/3 oz glucose
pinch of cream of tartar

Put all the ingredients, except the glucose and cream of tartar, into a large strong saucepan. Stir over a low heat until the sugar has dissolved, then boil the mixture steadily for 2-3 minutes. Blend in the glucose and cream of tartar and continue to boil steadily, stirring from time to time, until the mixture reaches 'firm ball' stage, or 121 C/250 F for a soft caramel. If you prefer a harder caramel, boil until the 'light crack' stage, 129 C/265 F. Do not beat the mixture, it should not be cloudy like fudge.

Grease a 20-cm/8-in square sandwich tin with a little butter; pour in the mixture. Allow to cool and become partially set then mark into sections. Leave in the tin until quite cold, cut neatly with a sharp knife then wrap each caramel in waxed paper.

Variations
Butter Caramels: use the ingredients above but melt 75 g/3 oz butter with the sugar mixture.
Creamy Chocolate Caramels: increase the amount of ordinary milk to 300 ml/½ pint. Break 175 g/6 oz plain chocolate into small pieces; add to the mixture with the glucose and cream of tartar. Since chocolate helps to set the sweet, allow the mixture to reach only 'slightly firm ball' stage, or 120 C/248 F, for a really soft caramel.
Creamy Coffee Caramels: use 150 ml/¼ pint strong black coffee instead of the ordinary milk in the recipe above.
Opera Caramels: use raspberry essence instead of vanilla and colour the mixture pale pink.

Caramelled Fruits (page 51)

RUSSIAN CARAMELS
Illustrated on page 41

---

*450 g/1 lb demerara sugar
1 (397-g/14-oz) can sweetened
condensed milk
100 g/4 oz butter
1 teaspoon vanilla essence*

Put all the ingredients into a strong saucepan; stir over a low heat until the sugar has dissolved. Boil steadily, stirring from time to time until the mixture reaches 'firm ball' stage, 121 C/250 F. This should be a soft type of caramel, but if you prefer a firmer sweet, boil to the 'light crack' stage, 129 C/265 F.

Grease a 20-cm/8-in square sandwich tin with a little butter; pour in the mixture. Allow to cool and become partially set then mark into sections. Leave in the tin until quite cold, cut neatly with a sharp knife then wrap each caramel in waxed paper.

TOASTED COCONUT CARAMELS
Illustrated on page 41

---

*450 g/1 lb caster sugar
150 ml/¼ pint water
pinch of cream of tartar
100 g/4 oz desiccated coconut*

Put the sugar, water and cream of tartar into a strong saucepan. Stir over a steady heat until the mixture reaches a 'fairly firm ball' stage or 118 C/245 F. Add the coconut and stir until the mixture becomes cloudy. Grease an 18-cm/7-in square sandwich tin with butter, pour in the mixture; when nearly cold cut into 2·5-cm/1-in squares. Leave in the tin until cold, remove and place on a large baking tray.

Toast under a preheated grill for a few seconds, turn and toast on the second, then on the third and fourth sides. Allow to cool then store in an airtight tin.

Brittles & Boiled Sweets

This chapter covers many traditional and favourite recipes, including Butterscotch, hard Brittle Nut Toffee and Buttered Brazils. Toffee Apples – always the children's favourite – are here and there is also a recipe for Sugared Almonds. The section on boiled sweets includes recipes for Mint Humbugs, Acid Drops, Fruit Drops and Barley Sugar Sticks. Children enjoy fruit lollies and you will find a recipe for these too. This type of sweet is not high in fat so it is quite suitable for children but care should be taken that a boiled sweet does not stick in the throat of a small child.

BUTTERSCOTCH

A good butterscotch, as the name suggests, should contain a high percentage of butter. This is heated with the sugar and water until it reaches the 'crack' stage. Recipes do vary; some contain milk, others glucose, others cream of tartar. The very high temperature to which one boils the mixture makes it essential to use a strong pan and to take care that it does not splash and become overheated. If the sugar mixture is boiled to too high a temperature, it turns dark in colour and bitter in flavour.

Wrap individual sweets in waxed paper and store in an airtight container. Reheating the sweet is only recommended if a sugar thermometer is used.

PLAIN BUTTERSCOTCH

Illustrated on page 44

450 g/1 lb granulated sugar
150 ml/¼ pint milk or double cream
3 tablespoons water
75 g/3 oz butter
pinch of cream of tartar

Put the ingredients into a strong saucepan and stir over a low heat until the sugar has dissolved. Boil steadily, stirring once or twice, until the mixture reaches 'crack' stage or 138 C/280 F.

Lightly grease a 23-cm/9-in square tin with melted butter. Pour in the butterscotch; when nearly set, mark into squares. Leave in the tin until cold then wrap in waxed paper.

BUTTERED BRAZILS OR WALNUTS

While the recipe for Plain Butterscotch can be used, the proportions below give a sweet that is better for coating.

15 Brazil nuts or 18 walnuts
25 g/1 oz glucose, preferably liquid type
225 g/8 oz granulated or demerara sugar
scant 150 ml/¼ pint water
25 g/1 oz butter

Place the nuts on a flat plate or tin and position near the cooker so they become slightly warmed. Put the glucose, sugar and water into a strong saucepan; stir over a low heat until the sugar has dissolved. Boil steadily until the mixture reaches 'hard crack' stage or 143 C/290 F; add the nuts and butter and blend with the mixture.

Lightly grease a flat tin with melted butter or oil. Lift the nuts out of the butterscotch, making quite certain they are thinly and evenly coated with the mixture. Place on the tin, allow to set, then wrap in waxed paper.

Acid Drops (page 53), Sugar Lollies (page 52), Toffee Apples (page 51) and Harlequin Humbugs (page 53)

PEANUT BRITTLE

Illustrated on page 44

The following recipe is particularly suitable for peanuts. Use fresh or salted nuts; if using fresh nuts blanch them first, omit salt with salted nuts.

450 g/1 lb granulated sugar
225 g/8 oz golden syrup
150 ml/¼ pint water
275 g/10 oz peanuts
¼ teaspoon salt
15 g/½ oz butter
¼ teaspoon bicarbonate of soda

Put the sugar, syrup and water into a large heavy saucepan, stir over a low heat until the sugar has dissolved. Boil until the mixture reaches the 'soft ball' stage or 114 C/238 F. Add the peanuts and salt, then continue to boil until the mixture reaches 'light crack' stage or 138 C/280 F; stir frequently during this stage. Add the butter and bicarbonate of soda, stir to blend; the mixture will bubble quite briskly.

Grease one or two large flat tins with melted butter or oil. Pour the mixture on to the tins then cool this partially by lifting around the edges with a metal spatula. Keep the spatula moving under the mixture so it does not stick to the tins. When it becomes firm but is still warm, turn the brittle over completely. Pull the edges to make the brittle thinner in the centre, allow to become quite cold, then break into pieces. Wrap in waxed paper.

Variation

Almond Brittle: omit the peanuts and salt in the recipe. Blanch 225-275 g/8-10 oz almonds and cut into narrow strips; add to the toffee mixture when it reaches 'light crack' stage. A few drops of almond or ratafia essence could be added.

Making Harlequin Humbugs

TOFFEE APPLES
Illustrated on page 49

8 dessert apples
225 g/8 oz granulated sugar
225 g/8 oz golden syrup

Choose ripe and perfect dessert apples that are not too large; the ideal apples are sweet and crisp in texture. Inspect the fruit carefully to see there are no bruises.

Before starting to make the toffee apples, assemble all the ingredients and equipment needed. Wash and dry the apples, but do not peel; insert the wooden sticks. Fill a large container with boiling water in which to stand the saucepan of cooked toffee so it does not harden in the pan; check that the container used is suitable to withstand the great heat of the toffee and saucepan. Prepare a basin of cold water for testing the toffee and a bowl of cold water in which to dip the coated apples so the toffee sets quickly. Finally, have a buttered baking tray on which to stand the toffee-coated apples.

Put the sugar and syrup into a strong saucepan and stir over a moderate heat until the sugar has dissolved. Boil until the mixture almost reaches the 'very hard crack' stage 154 C/310 F.

Dip the apples into the hot toffee and, if you want a thick coating, hold them over the pan for a moment then dip them again.

Unless the toffee apples are to be eaten immediately after the toffee coating is cold and set, or at least within an hour, it is essential to wrap them in waxed, grease-proof or cellophane paper. Secure the paper around the apples with a firm twist or an elastic band.

Variations
Medium Brittle Toffee: use 350 g/12 oz granulated sugar and 75 g/3 oz butter or margarine instead of the ingredients above. Follow the method of cooking as above, but boil only to 'hard crack' stage or 143 C/290 F. Coat the apples as above.

Creamy Toffee: use 450 g/1 lb demerara or granulated sugar, 50 g/2 oz butter, 150 ml/¼ pint single cream or milk, a pinch of cream of tartar and ½ tablespoon brown malt vinegar. Put all the ingredients into a strong saucepan, stir over a moderate heat until the sugar has dissolved. Boil steadily, stirring from time to time, until the mixture reaches 'hard crack' stage or 143 C/290 F. This recipe produces slightly more toffee than the two recipes above and will coat up to 10 apples.

Caramelled Fruits (illustrated on page 47): for a special occasion, try caramelising more unusual fruits and serve a selection of these at the end of a meal. The best to choose are grapes (remove the stalks, but not the pips) and seedless tangerines (peel and segment but do not remove the skin); strawberries when in season are also delicious. Lower the fruit into the syrup and turn carefully with two metal spoons until each piece is coated thinly but evenly. Lift out and place on a flat tin; leave until cold and hard then place into small petits fours cases.

SUGARED ALMONDS
Illustrated on page 59

It is not easy to make home cooked sugared almonds look as professional as those you can buy, but these are still very good to eat.

175 g/6 oz large almonds, blanched
450 g/1 lb loaf sugar
150 ml/¼ pint water
pinch of cream of tartar
colouring (optional)

After blanching the almonds dry them well, either by placing in a cool oven for a few minutes or by patting dry with absorbent kitchen paper. Arrange the nuts in a single flat layer in an ovenproof container and keep warm near the cooker. Cover the container.

Put the sugar, water and cream of tartar into a strong saucepan, stir over a low heat until the sugar has dissolved. Boil until the mixture reaches a firm 'soft ball', 116 C/240 F. Check the mixture carefully – if there is any scum on top remove this. Tint the sweet mixture if desired. Pour some of the very hot sugar mixture over the nuts; turn these in the mixture with two spoons or flat-bladed knives. Allow this layer to set. Re-boil the sugar mixture in the saucepan to the right stage again; add a second coating to the nuts. Allow to set once more (each coating takes about 10 minutes to set). Continue like this until the nuts are thickly coated and all the sugar mixture is used. Store in an airtight container.

Variations
Fondant Almonds: mould soft fondant around the blanched almonds (or other nuts).

Coloured Almonds: to achieve several colours, you will have to separate the sugar mixture into different pans, colouring each as required. Separate the almonds into the same number of ovenproof containers and pour a colour over each. Continue as above.

EDINBURGH ROCK
Illustrated on page 44

450 g/1 lb granulated or loaf sugar
200 ml/7 fl oz water
pinch of cream of tartar
flavourings and colourings; raspberry
essence and pink colouring, lemon essence
and saffron yellow colouring, peppermint
essence and green colouring

Put the sugar and water into a heavy saucepan; stir over a low heat until the sugar has dissolved. Boil steadily until the mixture reaches 'light crack' stage or 129 C/265 F; this is a little softer than butterscotch. Add the cream of tartar, stir well; allow to cool in the saucepan until the mixture thickens very slightly.

Brush two or three large flat tins with melted butter or oil; divide the mixture into two or three portions and place each on a tin. As soon as it is sufficiently cool to handle add the flavouring and colouring; knead into the mixture until evenly blended.

Dust the slab and your fingers with icing sugar and pull and knead each section of sweet until it becomes rather dull. When you have made really long thin sticks, cut into lengths of about 13 cm/5 in.

Leave at room temperature until the rock becomes quite powdery and soft. This will take up to a day in warm weather and a little longer if the weather is cold.

BRITTLE NUT TOFFEE

450 g/1 lb granulated sugar
150 ml/¼ pint milk
225 g/8 oz butter
225 g/8 oz nuts, blanched and chopped
(almonds, Brazil nuts, cashews, hazelnuts,
peanuts, pecan nuts, walnuts or
mixed nuts)

Put the ingredients, except the nuts, into a strong saucepan, stir over a moderate heat until the sugar dissolves. Boil fairly briskly until the mixture reaches 'hard crack' stage or 143 C/290 F. Add the nuts just before the mixture reaches this stage.

Lightly grease a flat tin with a little butter or oil. Drop spoonfuls of the nut toffee on to the tin and allow to set. If preferred use several kinds of nuts; put these into individual greased tins and quickly pour over the hot toffee. Leave until firm then break into pieces. Wrap in waxed paper to store or keep in an airtight tin.

BARLEY SUGAR STICKS
Illustrated on page 44

450 g/1 lb granulated or loaf sugar
150 ml/¼ pint water
few drops saffron yellow colouring
½ tablespoon lemon juice

Put all the ingredients into a strong saucepan; stir over a moderate heat until the sugar has dissolved. Boil steadily, without stirring, until the mixture reaches 'brittle' stage or 156 C/312 F.

Grease a slab or tin with a very little oil or melted butter. Allow the mixture to cool a little so it becomes slightly sticky then pour on to the slab or tin. Leave until cool enough to handle, then pull into very long thin strips. Twist these into the familiar barley sugar sticks. Wrap in waxed paper or cellophane.

Variations
Barley Sugar Sweets: use the recipe above but instead of twisting the sweet, pour into a 20-cm/8-in square oiled or buttered tin. Mark into neat pieces when half set.
Glucose Barley Sugar: follow the basic recipe above but use 225 g/8 oz sugar and 225 g/8 oz liquid glucose.
Lemon Barley Sugar: follow the recipe for Barley Sugar Sticks but add the thinly pared rind (use only the top yellow zest) of 1 large lemon to the sugar and water. Remove rind before 'brittle' stage is reached.

SUGAR LOLLIES
Illustrated on pages 11 and 49

Children love a sugared sweet on a stick. Choose any of the boiled sweet recipes. Allow the mixture to cook, as in the recipe, then to cool slightly, so it can be handled. Take out small amounts and mould these into rounds; insert a wooden stick into the mixture, then mould again to make a flattish round or oval shape. Leave to set hard on a marble slab or laminated board. Alternatively, put spoonfuls of the warm mixture on to a marble slab, shape into an oval and insert a wooden stick into each. Leave to set hard. Wrap the lollies in waxed paper or cellophane so they do not get over-sticky.

MINT HUMBUGS

450 g/1 lb demerara sugar
150 ml/¼ pint water
50 g/2 oz butter
½-¾ teaspoon peppermint essence or a
few drops oil of peppermint
pinch of cream of tartar

Put all the ingredients into a strong saucepan and stir over a low heat until the sugar has dissolved. Boil steadily, stirring once or twice, until the mixture reaches 'hard crack' stage, 143 C/290 C. Allow the mixture to cool a very little so it becomes slightly sticky.

Grease a slab or tin with a very little oil or melted butter. Pour the mixture on to the slab or tin, leave until cool enough to handle then pull into long strips. When cold cut into small pieces. Wrap and store.

Variations
Raspberry Humbugs: follow the recipe for Mint Humbugs but use granulated sugar and raspberry essence with pink colouring. To make striped Raspberry Humbugs (illustrated on page 53), colour only half the mixture, then twist the two strips together for a striped effect.

Shaded Mint Humbugs: use the recipe for Mint Humbugs but pull half the mixture rather more vigorously so it is a little paler in colour. Put the pale strip and the dark strip together and roll up so you have a slightly striped effect.

Harlequin Humbugs (illustrated on page 49): omit the peppermint, make the sweet and divide into two or three portions. Work various flavourings and colourings into each portion, pull these to form long strips then twist together for a striped effect. Cut into pieces.

ACID DROPS
Illustrated on page 49

450 g/1 lb granulated or loaf sugar
150 ml/¼ pint water
7 g/¼ oz tartaric acid, sifted

Put the sugar and water into a strong saucepan; stir over a moderate heat until the sugar has dissolved. Boil steadily, without stirring, until the mixture reaches 'brittle' stage, or 156 C/312 F. During the boiling stage skim the mixture (i.e. remove any grey bubbles that rise to the top) for the scum will spoil the clarity of the sweet.

Allow to cool slightly in the saucepan but while it is still of a pouring consistency add the tartaric acid. Mix thoroughly.

Raspberry Humbugs (left)

There are two ways of shaping the sweets. Either pour into individual ungreased tiny moulds and allow to set, or allow the mixture to cool until it can be handled then form into long bars and cut into individual portions.

Acid drops can be rolled in a little sifted icing sugar or wrapped individually in cellophane.

Variations
Fruit Drops: use the recipe for Acid Drops but work in a few drops of raspberry, lemon or orange essence with appropriate colourings, as well as the tartaric acid.

Fresh Fruit Drops: use the recipe for Acid Drops but omit the tartaric acid. Instead of water use fresh apple, grapefruit, orange or pineapple juice. You can also use a smooth fruit purée, such as sieved cooked rhubarb, sieved uncooked raspberries or strawberries instead of the juice. This does not produce such a clear sweet, but the flavour is excellent. Diluted blackcurrant syrup could also be used.

Fudge, Candy & Nougat

Fudge, candy and nougat are some of the most successful sweets to make at home. Their success depends upon using rather rich ingredients, such as butter and cream, or full-cream canned milk. Often less high-class ingredients are used in the commercial versions of these sweets in order to reduce the cost.

Fudge and candy are rather similar, but the texture is different. Fudge must be smooth, creamy and opaque (caused by beating the hot mixture); whereas candy, while having a creamy taste, is crisp, crumbly and clearer in appearance (the mixture is not beaten like fudge).

Nougat is an exotic sweetmeat that comes from the Middle East and France. Good nougat should not be too hard; it can seem slightly hard as you begin to eat it, then it should soften and become deliciously creamy, a perfect contrast to the firmness of the nuts it contains.

FUDGE

Fudge is a soft creamy sweet that is a favourite with most people. Unless you are preparing fudge for a special occasion such as a 'bring and buy' sale, it is better to make it in relatively small amounts, as in the recipes, so the mixture can be stirred and beaten efficiently in the saucepan.

The recipes for making fudge vary in the proportions used, but the mixture should contain butter as well as milk and/or cream or full-cream evaporated (un-sweetened) canned milk or full-cream condensed (sweetened) canned milk. Its success depends upon using these rather rich ingredients, although certain commercial versions tend to skimp on them in order to reduce the cost.

Because of the high cream or milk content, fudge has a tendency to burn in the pan and it must be stirred from time to time; the nearer the mixture gets to the 'soft ball' stage, the more it is inclined to stick to the pan and the more it should be stirred. Although you must boil to the correct temperature given in the recipes, take care not to exceed this, otherwise you will lose the soft creamy texture of the fudge. 114·4 C/238 F is the average temperature for fudge to set, but if you are making the fudge in very hot weather, then boil to 115·5 C/240 F, to be sure it will set in the greater heat.

You must beat fudge until it turns slightly cloudy in the pan, otherwise it may well become granular (sugary).

Store away from excess heat or dampness otherwise the fudge will become sticky looking on the outside. Keep in an airtight container to prevent it hardening and losing its soft texture; it can become rather hard with prolonged storage.

A variety of ingredients can be added to fudge (nuts, dried fruit etc) and it can be coated with chocolate, although it is too sweet for a fondant coating.

Raspberry Noyeau (page 63), Nougat Montélimar (page 63) and Chocolate Walnut Panocha (page 58) with Chiffon Fudge (page 57)

VANILLA FUDGE

An economical recipe.

450 g/1 lb granulated sugar
300 ml/½ pint milk
50 g/2 oz butter or margarine
½-1 teaspoon vanilla essence

Put the ingredients into a strong saucepan. Stir over a low heat until the sugar has dissolved. Boil steadily, stirring only occasionally (to prevent the mixture burning), until the fudge reaches 'soft ball' stage or 114 C/238 F. Remove the pan from the heat and beat until the mixture just *begins* to thicken and becomes opaque (cloudy) in appearance. This is very important when making fudge.

Grease a 20-cm/8-in square sandwich tin with a little melted butter or oil. Pour in the fudge and leave until almost set; cut into neat pieces with a sharp knife. Leave in the tin until quite firm. Fudge does not need wrapping in waxed paper, although this can be done if preferred.

Note This recipe produces a fudge that is pleasant to eat, but which lacks the creamy texture of richer recipes. It tends to harden slightly with prolonged storage and becomes almost like a candy.

CREAMY VANILLA FUDGE

450 g/1 lb granulated sugar
1 (397-g/14-oz) can sweetened condensed milk
50 g/2 oz butter or margarine
150 ml/¼ pint water
½-1 teaspoon vanilla essence

Put all the ingredients into a strong saucepan. Stir over a low heat until the sugar has dissolved. Boil steadily, stirring only occasionally (to prevent the mixture burning), until the fudge reaches 'soft ball' stage or 114 C/238 F. Remove the pan from the heat and beat until the mixture just begins to thicken and becomes opaque (cloudy) in appearance.

Grease a 20-cm/8-in square sandwich tin with a little melted butter or oil. Pour in the fudge and leave until almost set; cut into neat pieces with a sharp knife. Leave in the tin until quite firm.

Variations on Vanilla Fudge and Creamy Vanilla Fudge

Almond Fudge: use almond instead of vanilla essence. Chop 50 g/2 oz blanched almonds; add to the fudge when setting point is nearly reached.

Cherry Fudge: use the vanilla essence as in the recipe. Chop 50-100 g/2-4 oz glacé cherries; add these when setting point is nearly reached.

Chocolate Fudge: blend 2 tablespoons cocoa powder, 4 tablespoons drinking chocolate powder, or 75-100 g/3-4 oz chopped plain chocolate into the mixture when the sugar has melted.

Coffee Fudge: use 150 ml/¼ pint strong black coffee and 150 ml/¼ pint milk instead of the milk in Vanilla Fudge, or 150 ml/¼ pint strong black coffee instead of the water in Creamy Vanilla Fudge.

Ginger Fudge: omit the vanilla essence. Chop 50-100 g/2-4 oz crystallised or well-drained preserved ginger. Add this with 1 teaspoon ground ginger to the fudge just before setting point is reached.

Nut Fudge: any nuts can be added to fudge, using 50-175 g/2-6 oz. These should be skinned where possible, chopped and added just before setting point is reached.

Orange Fudge: omit the vanilla essence. Add the finely grated rind of 2 oranges with 50-100 g/2-4 oz chopped candied orange peel; add to the fudge just before setting point is reached.

Raisin Fudge: add approximately 100 g/4 oz seedless raisins just before setting point is reached.

Making Fudge

CHIFFON FUDGE
Illustrated on page 55

450 g/1 lb caster sugar or icing sugar, sifted
150 ml/¼ pint milk
150 ml/¼ pint double cream
25 g/1 oz butter
½ teaspoon vanilla essence

Put all the ingredients into a strong saucepan. Stir over a low heat until the sugar has dissolved. Boil steadily, stirring only occasionally (to prevent the mixture burning), until the fudge reaches 'soft ball' stage or 114 C/238 F. Remove the pan from the heat and beat until the mixture just begins to thicken and becomes opaque (cloudy) in appearance.

Grease a 20-cm/8-in square sandwich tin with a little melted butter or oil. Pour in the fudge and leave until almost set; cut into neat pieces with a sharp knife. Leave in the tin until quite firm.

Variation
Coconut Chiffon Fudge: add 100 g/4 oz desiccated coconut just before the 'soft ball' stage is reached.

OLD-FASHIONED CHOCOLATE FUDGE

450 g/1 lb granulated sugar
150 ml/¼ pint single cream or milk
100 g/4 oz bitter chocolate
1 tablespoon golden syrup
50 g/2 oz butter
½-1 teaspoon vanilla essence
walnut halves (optional)

Put all the ingredients, except the walnuts, into a strong saucepan and stir over a low heat until the sugar has dissolved. Boil steadily, stirring only occasionally (to prevent the mixture burning), until the fudge reaches 'soft ball' stage or 114 C/238 F. Remove the pan from the heat and beat until the mixture just begins to thicken and becomes opaque (cloudy) in appearance.

Grease a 20-cm/8-in square sandwich tin with a little melted butter or oil, and pour in the fudge. When the fudge just begins to set in the tin, mark it into neat pieces with a sharp knife and press a walnut half into each portion if desired. Leave in the tin until quite firm.

LUXURY MOCHA FUDGE

450 g/1 lb granulated sugar
300 ml/½ pint double cream
50 g/2 oz butter
150 ml/¼ pint strong black coffee
225 g/8 oz plain chocolate

Put all the ingredients, except the chocolate, into a strong saucepan, stir very carefully over a low heat until the sugar has dissolved. Break the chocolate into pieces then add to the sugar mixture. Boil steadily, stirring only occasionally (to prevent the mixture burning), until the fudge reaches 'soft ball' stage or 114 C/238 F. Remove the pan from the heat and beat until the mixture just begins to thicken and becomes opaque (cloudy) in appearance.

Grease a 20-cm/8-in square sandwich tin with a little melted butter or oil. Pour in the fudge and leave until almost set; cut into neat pieces with a sharp knife. Leave in the tin until quite firm.

PANOCHA

This is very like fudge, but the mixture is richer and darker because demerara sugar is used in place of most of the white sugar.

350 g/12 oz demerara sugar
100 g/4 oz granulated sugar
1 (170-g/6-oz) can evaporated milk
1 tablespoon golden syrup
1 tablespoon water
25 g/1 oz butter
½ teaspoon vanilla essence
50-100 g/2-4 oz mixed nuts, chopped

Put all the ingredients, except the nuts, into a strong saucepan and stir over a low heat until the sugars have dissolved. Boil steadily, stirring from time to time, until the mixture reaches 'soft ball' stage or 114 C/238 F. Add the nuts, remove from the heat and beat until cloudy.

Grease a 20-cm/8-in square sandwich tin with a little melted butter or oil. Pour in the panocha and leave until almost set; cut into neat pieces with a sharp knife. Leave in the tin until quite firm.

Variations

Barbados Pineapple Panocha: use 225 g/8 oz Barbados (moist brown) sugar and 225 g/8 oz granulated sugar, 1 (170-g/6-oz) can evaporated milk, 50 g/2 oz butter and 1 teaspoon vanilla essence. Drain and chop 100 g/4 oz canned pineapple.

Put all these ingredients into a strong saucepan, stir until the sugars have dissolved then boil steadily, stirring from time to time, until the 'soft ball' stage or 114 C/238 F is reached. Chop 100 g/4 oz walnuts, stir into the mixture and beat until cloudy. Continue as above.

Chocolate Walnut Panocha (illustrated on page 55): follow the basic recipe but add 50 g/2 oz plain chocolate to the sugar mixture when it has melted. Use chopped walnuts in place of mixed nuts.

Marzipan Fruits (page 68) and Sugared Almonds (page 71)

CANDY

The ingredients used and the method of making candy and fudge are somewhat similar. The difference is that fudge is essentially soft and creamy whereas candy is always crisper and firmer in texture. While some special candy recipes are more economical than those used for fudge, it is quite possible to take a fudge recipe and make candy from it. The different texture is achieved by boiling the mixture to a slightly higher temperature, that is 115·5 C/240 F instead of 114·4 C/238 F, and maintaining the mixture at this temperature for one or two minutes. The different appearance of candy – clear rather than the cloudy look of fudge – is caused by the fact that a candy mixture is not beaten in the saucepan before being poured into the greased tin to set.

Candy can dry so much with keeping that it becomes crumb-like and can break into pieces very easily. Store in an airtight tin and away from excess heat.

BAKED NUT CANDY

2 egg whites
225 g/8 oz demerara sugar
½ teaspoon vanilla essence
100 g/4 oz mixed nuts, finely chopped

Whisk the egg whites until very stiff, gradually beat in the sugar then fold in the vanilla essence and nuts. Lightly oil one or two non-stick baking trays or use silicone (non-stick) paper to line ordinary baking trays.

Put teaspoons of the mixture on the trays then bake on the coolest oven setting (90-110 C, 200-225 F, gas 0-¼) for 1-1¼ hours. Cool and pack in airtight containers.

Variations
Chocolate Nut Candy: blend 50 g/2 oz drinking chocolate powder with the sugar.
Coffee Nut Candy: blend 1-2 teaspoons instant coffee powder with the sugar.

VANILLA CANDY

1 (397-g/14-oz) can sweetened condensed milk
water (see below)
50 g/2 oz butter or margarine
1 teaspoon vanilla essence
450 g/1 lb granulated sugar

Pour the condensed milk into the saucepan; fill the can with water, add this to the condensed milk together with the butter or margarine, vanilla essence and sugar. Stir over a low heat until the sugar has dissolved, then boil steadily, stirring only occasionally until the mixture reaches the 'soft ball' stage, 116 C/240 F, but very slightly firmer than for fudge. If you like a softish candy remove the pan from the heat at once; if you prefer a crisper sweet, boil slowly (so the temperature will not rise) for 1-2 minutes.

Grease a 20-cm/8-in square tin with a little butter or margarine. Pour in the unbeaten mixture, allow to become almost cold, then mark into squares.

Variations
Butterscotch Candy: use 350 g/12 oz brown (preferably demerara) sugar and 100 g/4 oz golden syrup instead of granulated sugar.
Chocolate Candy: use only ½ teaspoon vanilla essence; add 50 g/2 oz sifted cocoa powder or 100 g/4 oz drinking chocolate powder or 100 g/4 oz chopped plain chocolate to the mixture when the sugar has dissolved and the mixture reaches boiling point.
Coconut Candy: add 175 g/6 oz desiccated or finely grated fresh coconut to the mixture when the sugar has dissolved.
Nut Candy: chop 100-175 g/4-6 oz nuts; add to the mixture just before the 'soft ball' stage is reached.

Nougat Montélimar (page 63)

Nougat or Noyeau

Nougat is an exotic sweetmeat that comes from the Middle East and France. Good nougat should not be too hard; it can seem slightly hard as you begin to eat it, then it should soften and become deliciously creamy, a perfect contrast to the firmness of the nuts it contains.

Nougat is not particularly difficult to make but it needs careful attention to the various stages of heating. The traditional method is to boil together sugar and water with golden syrup until it reaches the 'firm to very firm ball' stage (121-132 C/250-270 F) then add whisked egg whites, warmed honey and nuts. Make sure the sugar mixture has reached the temperature given in the recipe before it is incorporated with the whisked egg whites and beat all the time while adding it to the egg whites. The inclusion of golden syrup and honey makes the deliciously 'chewy' type of nougat.

It is traditional to put nougat between sheets of rice paper, then wrap individual pieces in waxed or greaseproof paper. Store in airtight tins or boxes, as it does tend to become hard if exposed to the air.

Nougat can be coated with chocolate but is usually left plain.

Golden Nougat

This is a very sweet chewy nougat.

450 g/1 lb granulated sugar
150 ml/¼ pint water
3 tablespoons golden syrup
pinch of cream of tartar
3 tablespoons honey
4 egg whites
100 g/4 oz pistachio nuts, blanched
and chopped
few drops vanilla essence
To Coat and Cover:
rice paper or wafers

Put the sugar, water and golden syrup into a strong saucepan; stir over a moderate heat until the sugar has dissolved. Boil steadily until the mixture reaches 'very firm ball' stage or 132 C/270 F. Stir in the cream of tartar.

While the sugar and syrup mixture is boiling, put the honey into a saucepan over very low heat, or use the top of a double saucepan or a heatproof basin over boiling water. Heat until the honey is very hot. Put the egg whites into a large ovenproof mixing bowl and whisk until very stiff. Lift the mixing bowl over a saucepan of boiling water; gradually pour the golden syrup mixture on to the egg whites, stirring very well as you do so. When thoroughly blended, add the hot honey, chopped nuts and vanilla essence. Stir the mixture for a few minutes then test again. At this stage the nougat should be at 'firm ball' stage or 121 C/250 F (lower than the temperature initially).

If too soft continue to heat over the hot water and test again; never transfer the mixture to a saucepan. Line a 25-cm/10-in square tin with rice paper or ice cream wafers. Pour the mixture into the tin, cover with more rice paper or wafers. Allow to set, cut into neat pieces and wrap in waxed paper.

Whisking syrup into egg whites for nougat

Nougat Montélimar

Illustrated on pages 55 and 61

450 g/1 lb loaf or granulated sugar
40 g/1 ½ oz liquid glucose
150 ml/¼ pint water
350 g/12 oz honey, preferably clear
1 ½ large or 2 small egg whites
150 g/5 oz icing sugar, sifted
175 g/6 oz almonds, blanched and
coarsely chopped
50-100 g/2-4 oz pistachio nuts, blanched
and halved
100 g/4 oz glacé cherries, chopped
To Coat and Cover:
rice paper

Put the loaf sugar, glucose and water into a strong saucepan, stir over a low heat until the sugar has dissolved. Boil, without stirring, until the mixture reaches 'crack' stage or 138 C/280 F. While the sugar mixture is boiling, put the honey into a second saucepan and boil until it reaches 'firm ball' stage or 121 C/

250 F. Put the egg whites into an ovenproof mixing bowl, whisk until they are very stiff, then gradually pour the very hot sugar mixture on to the egg whites, beating all the time. When the sugar mixture has been incorporated beat in the hot honey and then the icing sugar. Finally add the nuts and cherries.

Line a 23-cm/9-in square tin with rice paper; pour in the hot nougat. Top with more rice paper, cool slightly, then cover the surface with a weight. Leave for 24 hours; cut into oblong shapes. Wrap in waxed paper and store in an airtight tin.

Raspberry Noyeau

Illustrated on page 55

This recipe needs the minimum of cooking but has the lightness of true nougat.

225 g/8 oz icing sugar, sifted
½ teaspoon raspberry essence
75 g/3 oz honey
½ tablespoon glucose
3 egg whites
175 g/6 oz almonds, blanched and chopped
50 g/2 oz glacé cherries, chopped
pink colouring (optional)
To Coat and Cover:
25 g/1 oz icing sugar, sifted
rice paper

Put the sugar, essence, honey and glucose into a large heatproof mixing bowl and stand over a saucepan of boiling water. Heat until the mixture is like a syrup. Whisk the egg whites in another bowl until very stiff, then add to the sugar mixture. Continue to beat over the heat until the sweet becomes very thick. Add the almonds and cherries and any colouring required. Allow to cool slightly.

Dust an 18-cm/7-in square tin with half the icing sugar, then cover the base with rice paper. Spoon in the nougat mixture, top with more rice paper and icing sugar. Put a light weight over the top and leave until cold, then cut into neat bars.

Pouring nougat mixture into a tin

Marshmallows, Turkish Delight & Jellies

Sweets such as Marshmallows and Turkish Delight are examples of jellied sweets. Although these sound simple to make, a certain amount of sugar boiling is necessary and care should be taken to see that the temperature given in the recipes is reached. Gelatine varies in strength, but the well-known powdered makes should give you the correct result if the amount in these recipes is used. In some recipes there is rather lengthy stirring of the mixture; this is very essential and must not be overlooked.

The jellied sweets will keep in good condition if well dredged in icing sugar. If coating in chocolate, make quite certain that the chocolate has become cold so it cannot melt the sweets. As they keep well, it is worthwhile making a good quantity at one time. Pack in layers in boxes or tins; each layer should be covered with plenty of sifted icing sugar.

MARSHMALLOWS

275 g/10 oz loaf or granulated sugar
150 ml/¼ pint water plus 4 tablespoons
4 tablespoons orange flower water or
2 tablespoons lemon juice
½ tablespoon glucose
20 g/¾ oz gelatine
1 egg white
40 g/1½ oz icing sugar, sifted
To Coat:
25 g/1 oz icing sugar, sifted

Put the sugar, 150 ml/¼ pint of the water, the orange flower water or lemon juice and the glucose into a strong saucepan. Stir over a low heat until the sugar has melted. Boil steadily until the mixture reaches 'firm ball' stage or 127 C/260 F.

Meanwhile, put the remaining water into a basin, sprinkle the gelatine on top, leave to soften for a few minutes then stand over a pan of very hot water until the gelatine has dissolved. Blend the dissolved gelatine into the sugar mixture.

Whisk the egg white until stiff in a large heatproof basin, then pour the hot sugar and gelatine mixture on to the egg white. Beat vigorously until the mixture begins to stiffen.

Line the base and sides of a 20-cm/8-in square tin with waxed or greaseproof paper. Sprinkle about 25 g/1 oz of the icing sugar over the paper. Pour the marshmallow mixture into the tin. Cover with the remaining icing sugar, then waxed or greaseproof paper and quite a heavy weight; this needs to give even pressure over the entire surface of the sweet.

Allow to cool then cut into neat pieces with kitchen scissors. Roll in icing sugar to coat. Leave the marshmallows in the air for at least 24 hours until the outside hardens, then pack in an airtight container.

Note The mixture can be tinted if desired.

Variation
Raspberry Marshmallows: use sieved uncooked raspberry purée instead of water in the recipe above. Cooked apricot purée or uncooked strawberry purée also make delicious marshmallows.

Uncooked Coconut Ice (page 72), Turkish Delight (page 66), Stuffed Dates (page 68) and Cherry Balls (page 71)

TURKISH DELIGHT 1

Illustrated on page 65

A fairly quick recipe.

450 g/1 lb loaf sugar
300 ml/½ pint water
25 g/1 oz gelatine
4 tablespoons lemon juice
½ teaspoon tartaric acid
pink colouring
To Coat:
25 g/1 oz icing sugar, sifted

Put the sugar and all the water except 4 tablespoons into a strong saucepan; stir over a low heat until the sugar has dissolved. Soften the gelatine in the remaining cold water, add to the sugar mixture and stir until the gelatine has dissolved. Boil steadily for 8 minutes, stirring all the time, then add the lemon juice and tartaric acid.

Dampen two 15-cm/6-in square tins and pour half the mixture into one tin. Tint the remaining mixture a delicate pink and pour into the second tin. Allow the mixtures to set; cut into squares with a damp knife or kitchen scissors and roll in the icing sugar.

Variation

Crème de menthe Turkish Delight: add a few drops of peppermint essence to the mixture and tint it green instead of pink. For a more luxurious sweet, omit 4 tablespoons water and use 4 tablespoons crème de menthe liqueur; colouring is then unnecessary. If preferred, use the full amount of water, omit the lemon juice and substitute the crème de menthe.

TURKISH DELIGHT 2

This recipe does not contain gelatine but the prolonged cooking of the cornflour mixture produces a clear jellied appearance.

450 g/1 lb sugar
900 ml/1 ½ pints water
¼ teaspoon tartaric acid
200 g/7 oz icing sugar, sifted
75 g/3 oz cornflour
2 tablespoons lemon juice
50 g/2 oz honey
pink colouring
To Coat:
25 g/1 oz icing sugar, sifted

This is less easy than the previous recipe, but it does produce a better taste. The cloudy cornflour mixture becomes clear with prolonged cooking.

Put the sugar and 150 ml/¼ pint of the water into a strong saucepan, stir over a low heat until the sugar has dissolved, then allow to boil steadily until 'soft ball' stage or 116 C/240 F; add the tartaric acid.

Blend the icing sugar and cornflour with the rest of the cold water and pour into a second saucepan. Bring to the boil, stirring all the time, and boil until the mixture thickens. Add the syrup from the first saucepan to the cornflour mixture, then add the lemon juice. Boil steadily for 25-30 minutes in an uncovered pan until the mixture is straw-coloured and clear; stir frequently during this time. Add the honey, stir well to blend.

Lightly oil two 18-cm/7-in square tins or brush with a very little butter. Pour half the mixture into one tin. Tint the remaining mixture pale pink and pour into the second tin. Allow the mixture to set then cut into squares and roll in the icing sugar.

Variation

Chocolate Turkish Delight: pour the mixture into a number of small oblong, square or round moulds or patty tins. Leave until firm, turn out and then coat with cooled melted chocolate.

Making Turkish Delight

APPLE SQUARES

Illustrated on page 27

1 kg/2 lb cooking apples
300 ml/½ pint water
granulated sugar (see method)
gelatine (see method)
lemon juice (see method)
To Coat:
25 g/1 oz icing sugar, sifted, or caster sugar

Wash and slice the apples; do not peel or core if you intend to sieve the fruit. If using a liquidiser then the peel and cores must be removed. Simmer the fruit in the water until soft. Sieve or liquidise and return to the saucepan. Cook gently, stirring from time to time, until a very stiff purée. Measure this and to each 600 ml/ 1 pint purée allow 450 g/1 lb sugar, 40 g/1½ oz gelatine, ½ tablespoon lemon juice and 2 tablespoons water.

Return the purée to the pan, add the sugar and stir over a low heat until dissolved. Boil steadily, stirring from time to time, until the mixture reaches 'very soft ball' stage or 113 C/236 F. Soften the gelatine in the lemon juice and cold water, add to the sugar mixture and dissolve over a very low heat.

Lightly oil a 20-cm/8-in square tin, pour in the mixture then allow to set. Cut into squares with a damp knife or kitchen scissors. Roll in the sugar.

Variations
Apple Nut Squares: chop 100 g/4 oz nuts, add to the apple mixture just before 'soft ball' stage is reached.
Apricot Squares: soak 225 g/8 oz dried apricots in 1·15 litres/2 pints cold water for 12 hours. Simmer the fruit in this water until soft, then proceed as Apple Squares above. 1-2 tablespoons apricot brandy could be added to each 600 ml/1 pint purée.
Apricot Almond Squares: chop 100 g/4 oz blanched almonds, add to the apricot mixture, just before the 'soft ball' stage is reached.

FRENCH JELLIES

450 g/1 lb granulated or loaf sugar
225 ml/7½ fl oz water
¼ teaspoon citric acid or 2 tablespoons lemon juice
20 g/¾ oz gelatine
flavouring (see method)
colouring (see method)
To Coat:
25 g/1 oz icing sugar, sifted

Put the sugar and 150 ml/¼ pint of the water into a strong saucepan and stir over a moderate heat until the sugar dissolves. Add the citric acid or lemon juice, boil until the mixture reaches 'soft ball' stage or 114 C/ 238 F.

Soften the gelatine in the remaining cold water, add to the mixture in the saucepan and boil for 2-3 minutes. Pour the mixture into heatproof small containers. Add various flavouring essences, lemon, raspberry, rum etc; colour the mixtures accordingly. Dampen small tins, pour in the mixtures and allow to set. Cut into squares with a damp knife or kitchen scissors and roll in the icing sugar.

Variations
Fruit Jellies: use undiluted fruit juice, such as grapefruit, orange or pineapple, instead of the water in the recipe above, or use diluted blackcurrant syrup. The citric acid or lemon juice can be omitted or reduced in quantity. Unfortunately the very high temperature to which the mixture is boiled does destroy the vitamin content, but the jellies taste delicious.
Ginger Jellies: use only half the amount of citric acid or lemon juice in the basic recipe; add 1 teaspoon ground ginger to the sugar. When the sweet has reached 'soft ball' stage or 114 C/238 F, remove from the heat. Chop 100-175 g/4-6 oz preserved ginger very finely, blend into the hot sugar mixture, then proceed as the basic recipe.

Uncooked Sweets

MARZIPAN FRUITS
Illustrated on pages 59 and 70

A box of marzipan fruits looks most attractive and they are not difficult to make. Dust the board and your fingers with a little sifted icing or caster sugar, so the marzipan does not become sticky. Below are some suggestions for simple fruits, but once you have acquired the knack of these, you will soon be trying out more ideas of your own.

Apples: colour the marzipan a pleasant apple green and form into the shape of tiny apples. Dip a very fine brush into pink colouring and shade one side, to look like a ripening apple. Press a clove into the base and a tiny angelica stalk into the top.

Bananas: colour the marzipan yellow like a banana. Form into tiny banana shapes. Dip a fine paint brush into either strongish coffee or rather thin diluted chocolate and brush on the brown marks of a banana.

Peaches: colour the marzipan a pinky yellow. Form into balls and then make into peach shapes. Dip a fine brush into pink colouring and shade like a peach.

Pears: colour the marzipan a pleasant yellowy-green and form into the shape of tiny pears. Dip a very fine brush into pink colouring and shade one side, to look like a ripening pear. Press a clove into the base and tiny angelica stalk into the top.

Strawberries: colour the marzipan a very delicate pinky red with cochineal and 2-3 drops of saffron yellow so it is not too mauvy-red in colour. Form into strawberry shapes and top with tiny green marzipan stalks and/or leaf shapes. Make tiny indentations with a fine needle on the strawberries and dip in sugar.

Lemons: colour the marzipan lemon yellow and form into small lemon shapes. Press a clove into the base of each and roll the lemon gently over a nutmeg grater to give the correct texture to the skin.

Cherries: colour the marzipan red with cochineal, adding 1-2 drops of yellow if necessary. Shape into small balls the size of a cherry and stick a green angelica stalk into each.

Easy Sweets with Marzipan

Marzipan Fudge: make any of the fudge recipes. Make marzipan with 225 g/8 oz ground almonds etc. The marzipan using equal quantities of ground almonds and sugar is a good choice for this recipe, since it is not too sweet. Roll out the marzipan to fit a fairly deep and lightly oiled 20-cm/8-in tin, top with the fudge, allow to set then cut into squares or fingers. The two delicate sweets blend well.

Neapolitan Bars: divide the marzipan into three or four portions. Tint each portion a different colour. Roll out to equal-sized rectangles, then place one portion on top of another until you have three or four layers. Cut into small fingers and roll in caster, granulated or sifted icing sugar while still soft.

Stuffed Dates (illustrated on page 65): remove the stones from dates and fill with marzipan. Roll in caster sugar if liked.

Stuffed Dates, Cherries and Walnuts (page 71)

UNCOOKED MARZIPAN OR ALMOND PASTE

This is the classic uncooked mixture, used to coat cakes, as well as being a sweet; it has an excellent flavour and is not too sweet.

225 g/8 oz ground almonds
100 g/4 oz caster sugar
100 g/4 oz icing sugar, sifted
few drops ratafia or almond essence
2 small or 1 large egg yolk(s)

Mix all the ingredients together; knead lightly and use.

Variations

Use slightly less egg yolk and add sweet or dry sherry or a liqueur to bind. Delicious for the centre of chocolates.

To give a lighter colour to the marzipan, which makes it ideal for tinting to form into flowers or fruits, bind the mixture with egg white rather than egg yolk.

Economical Marzipan: this uses less of the expensive ground almonds and makes a marzipan that is easy to handle. Blend together 450 g/1 lb sifted icing sugar, 225 g/8 oz ground almonds, a few drops of almond or ratafia essence and 1 teaspoon liquid glucose. Bind with 1½-2 whole eggs or use just egg yolks or egg whites, if preferred.

Making Marzipan Fruits (page 68)

UNCOOKED FONDANT

Fondant can be used as a sweet by itself or as a filling. Various colourings and flavourings can be added to fondant or it may be mixed with nuts or glacé fruits.

450 g/1 lb icing sugar, sifted
2 egg whites
½ tablespoon lemon juice
colouring and flavouring

Put the ingredients into a basin and beat until a stiff smooth mixture. If the egg whites are rather small you may need a little extra lemon juice or water to give the correct consistency.

If using an electric mixer choose a low speed. If using a food processor allow only about 25 seconds processing.

Add colouring and flavouring as in the individual recipes.

Note To make a softer fondant add 1-2 teaspoons glycerine or liquid glucose.

Variation

Sift 450 g/1 lb icing sugar and blend it with approximately 5 tablespoons sweetened condensed canned milk; add this gradually to achieve the desired consistency. Add colouring and flavouring as desired. This is a softer and stickier fondant than the basic recipe above.

Simple Sweets from Fondant

Almond Creams: add a few drops of almond essence and colouring to the fondant, roll into small balls, flatten and top with blanched almonds.

Cherry Balls (illustrated on page 65): chop 100-175 g/4-6 oz glacé cherries, add to the fondant, mix thoroughly then roll into balls. Add a few drops of cochineal to colour pink if liked.

Coconut Balls or Squares: add 50 g/2 oz desiccated coconut to the fondant, roll into balls or shape into squares, then roll in desiccated coconut. The coconut for the coating could be toasted until a golden brown before use.

Stuffed Dates (illustrated on page 69): make the fondant a little softer than usual (by adding slightly more lemon juice) and tint it pale pink. Slit dessert dates, remove stones and fill with the fondant. As a variation to this, colour the fondant light green and use to fill stoned prunes.

Stuffed Cherries (illustrated on page 69): colour the fondant pale yellow, shape into small balls and use to sandwich together.

Stuffed Walnuts (illustrated on page 69): flavour and colour the fondant with a little melted chocolate and mould into small triangular shapes. Press three walnut halves into the sides.

Harlequin Shapes (illustrated on page 27): fondant can provide a complete selection of sweets if you add various colourings and flavourings to small batches of the mixture. Cut into fancy shapes, such as stars, hearts, diamonds, etc. Top the sweets with silver balls, crystallised rose petals, angelica, glacé cherries and nuts.

Sugar Mice: mould the fondant into an oval mouse shape and insert a piece of string into the wider end for the tail. Use currants for the eyes, halved flaked almonds for the ears, two small pieces of green angelica for the whiskers and a pink sugar dragee for the nose.

Sugared Almonds (illustrated on page 59): colour the fondant delicately, then mould it around blanched almonds.

Uncooked Coconut Ice

Illustrated on pages 27 and 65

Coconut ice is inclined to become dry and crumble if kept for too long a period. It can then be used as a cake filling or decoration; break it into pieces and blend with whipped cream.

5 tablespoons sweetened condensed milk
450 g/1 lb icing sugar, sifted
175 g/6 oz desiccated coconut
pink colouring

Mix together the condensed milk, all the icing sugar except 1 tablespoon, and the coconut. The mixture will be thick so should be mixed very vigorously. Remove half the mixture from the bowl; shape into a neat oblong. Add the colouring to the remaining mixture, blend well then shape into another oblong, identical to the first. Put on to the white oblong; press together firmly. Dust a flat tin with the remaining icing sugar. Place the coconut ice on this, leave until firm then cut into neat slices.

Variation
Cream Coconut Ice: use double cream in place of condensed milk.

Uncooked Toffee

225 g/8 oz golden syrup
225 g/8 oz dried milk powder, preferably full-cream
1-2 teaspoons vanilla essence

Put the ingredients into a large heatproof basin over a pan of hot water. Heat only until the syrup has melted. Stir from time to time to blend the milk powder with the syrup. Remove from the heat and cool sufficiently to handle, then knead until smooth. Allow to cool but before the mixture becomes firm cut into pieces with a pair of sharp scissors or a knife.

Uncooked Vanilla Fudge

100 g/4 oz butter or margarine
100 g/4 oz granulated sugar
4 tablespoons golden syrup
¼- ½ teaspoon vanilla essence
12 tablespoons full-cream dried milk powder

Put all the ingredients except the dried milk powder into a saucepan and stir over a low heat until the sugar has dissolved. Remove from the heat and add the dried milk powder. Mix well with a spoon then with the fingertips.

Grease an 18-cm/7-in square tin with a little butter; press the mixture into the tin and allow to become quite cold, then mark into squares.

Variations
Uncooked Chocolate Fudge: add 100 g/4 oz plain chocolate to the dissolved sugar mixture; when the chocolate has melted, stir in the dried milk powder. Continue as above.
Uncooked Coffee Fudge: add 2 teaspoons instant coffee powder to the dissolved sugar mixture then stir in the dried milk powder. Continue as above.

Uncooked Chocolate Orange Nut Fudge

100 g/4 oz plain chocolate
50 g/2 oz butter
4 tablespoons evaporated canned milk
grated rind of 1 orange
100 g/4 oz mixed nuts, chopped
450 g/1 lb icing sugar, sifted

Break the chocolate into pieces, put into a heatproof basin with the butter and stand over a pan of hot, but not boiling, water until the chocolate has melted. Remove from the heat, add the milk, orange rind and nuts. Mix well then gradually work in the icing sugar.

Grease a shallow 19 x 29-cm/7½ x 11½-in tin with a little butter. Pour in the mixture, spread flat; allow to set then cut into squares.

UNCOOKED CHOCOLATE NUT FUDGE

225 g/8 oz plain chocolate
25 g/1 oz butter
1 egg
6 tablespoons sweetened condensed milk
450 g/1 lb icing sugar, sifted
100 g/4 oz mixed nuts, chopped
½ teaspoon vanilla essence

Break the chocolate into small pieces, put into a heatproof basin with the butter and egg. Stand over a pan of hot, but not boiling, water. Stir briskly, or whisk, until the chocolate has melted and the mixture is thick and creamy.

Add the remaining ingredients. Remove from the heat and beat the mixture until it becomes cloudy and begins to thicken.

Grease a 20-cm/8-in square sandwich tin with a little butter, pour in the mixture and leave for several hours until set, then mark into squares.

Making Peppermint Creams (page 23)

CHOCOLATE NUT CLUSTERS
Illustrated on page 22

To make perfectly shaped clusters you need to shape the nut and chocolate mixture while it is soft and pliable.

Melt the chocolate in a heatproof basin over a pan of very hot, but not boiling, water. Leave until just melted; do not overheat. Add the nuts; these can be whole peanuts, but blanched almonds should be cut into strips (flaked almonds are too thin to make good clusters); Brazils, cashew nuts and walnuts should be cut into fairly large pieces. Blend the nuts with the chocolate; you can use up to 175 g/6 oz nuts to each 225 g/8 oz chocolate. Take small spoonfuls of the soft mixture, put in little heaps on a lightly oiled tin. Take a clean knife to shape each heap into a slightly neater round. Allow to set.

To coat the nut clusters in chocolate, dip carefully on the end of a fine fork into melted chocolate. Place on waxed paper and leave to set.

PACKING & WRAPPING

Throughout this book emphasis has been given to the importance of wrapping chocolates and sweets and correct storage. There will be many occasions when you will be presenting homemade sweets as a gift, or making them to raise money for charity at a fête or bazaar. The finished appearance is then of great importance.

Wrapping Papers

Waxed paper is recommended in many recipes, for it is pliable and easy to fold around the sweets and it keeps them in good condition. However, it is not particularly attractive in appearance, and there are several other types of paper that could be used. These are obtainable from a good store or from stationers who specialise in cake and sweet containers.

Gold and silver wrapping paper is available but check when buying this that it is of the type suitable for contact with food; if doubtful, wrap the sweets first in waxed paper then in the metallic paper. You can buy coloured transparent-type paper, similar in texture to waxed paper, and fine Japanese wrapping papers. Clear or coloured cellophane paper also makes an attractive wrapping. To wrap sweets, cut neat squares or rounds and practise folding the paper around the sweet. Always have the joins on the base of the sweets.

Cases

Small paper cases (often called confectionery or petits fours cases) are sold in packets, either plain white, gold or silver, or with delicate patterns. The cases not only look attractive, but they help to support rather fragile chocolates and sweets.

Lining Paper

Containers for sweets and chocolates often need a lining paper. If you have a selection of different kinds of sweets, plain white or pale coloured paper looks most attractive. You could use large doilies or baking parchment (which is firm enough to cut neatly). Aluminium foil also makes a good lining for containers.

Containers

If you are presenting sweets or chocolates as a gift, there are many containers that can be used. The most obvious is to pack the sweets in boxes, but you may wish to add to the value of the present by using something of greater worth. People who collect interesting kitchenware would be delighted to have a French type of flan dish filled with chocolates or sweets.

Arrange these carefully, cover the whole container with cling film, then top with ribbon.

Small casseroles or other dishes could be filled in a similar way. Kitchen storage jars can also be filled with sweets; if you are giving a set of jars you could fill each with a different kind of sweet.

Filling Boxes

Gift boxes are sold in many stores and stationers, and the range available nowadays is very attractive. It is a good idea to buy the box or boxes before cutting the sweets into squares or other shapes; you will then know exactly how they will fit, for a box looks much more attractive if it is well-filled, but not overcrowded. Fairly large shallow boxes enable you to display more. If using boxes that have already contained chocolates or sweets, cover them with gold, silver or patterned wrapping paper.

First line the base and sides of the box; the lining paper should be sufficiently deep to form a cover over the top of the sweets when the box is full. Arrange the sweets or chocolates in the box. If you have a limited selection of two or three kinds, then they can be arranged as in commercial boxes, with a good distribution of shape, size and coloured wrappings. It is a sensible idea to have a neat card inside detailing the various kinds of sweets and chocolates and their position in the box. If you plan more than one layer, it is important to protect the first layer with a thick sheet of paper (or thin card covered with lining paper).

Top the filled boxes with a bow, or tie a length of ribbon attractively around the box.

Attractively packed sweets make a welcome gift

Index